AF560750

TRAINING THE TEACHER TRAINER

Strategies • Techniques • Modern Tools

TRAINING THE TEACHER TRAINER

Strategies • Techniques • Modern Tools

DIWAKAR SHARMA

Master of Mass Communication – Guru Jambeshwar University, Hisar
Postgraduate Certificate in Public Relations – Niagara College, Canada
Graduate Certificate in Teaching English as a Second Language – Niagara College, Canada
Bachelor of Business Administration – Ch. Charan Singh University, Meerut
Diploma in Tourism Studies – IGNOU
Certificate in Computing – IGNOU
Dean Academics, BLS Institute of Technology Management, Bahadurgarh, Haryana, India
(Affiliated to Guru Gobind Singh Indraprastha University, Delhi)

DEEP & DEEP PUBLICATIONS PVT. LTD.
F-159, Rajouri Garden, New Delhi - 110 027

TRAINING THE TEACHER TRAINER

Strategies • Techniques • Modern Tools

ISBN 978-81-8450-307-4

Printed in India at MAYUR ENTERPRISES
WZ Plot No. 3, Gujjar Market, Tihar Village, New Delhi - 110 018

Published by DEEP & DEEP PUBLICATIONS PVT. LTD.
F-159, Rajouri Garden, New Delhi - 110 027 • Phone : 25435369, 25440916
E-mail : ddpbooks@yahoo.co.in • ddpubs@gmail.com
Showroom :
2/13, Ansari Road, Daryaganj, New Delhi - 110 002 • Telefax : 23245122

Contents

Foreword

All around the world millions of learners enter schools and colleges for developing personality and gaining valuable knowledge. Teaching, teacher training, and understanding the need of the learner is extremely important for learners around the world. Teaching is considered as a very noble profession, and teachers are respected almost everywhere. The shine of this noble profession has started to diminish and the respect which teachers used to receive in the past is somewhat lost. The relationship between teacher's characteristics and their learner's achievement has been the major subject of various researches. Most of the researches focus on the impact of teacher salaries, experience and measures of teacher's pre-service training such as educational background.

Training plays an important role in the overall development of the learner, and the learning continues for the entire life. We the educators must be prepared to change with time and enrich our experience and enrol ourselves in faculty development programs. The effect of on-the-job or in-service training has received much less attention. Diwakar Sharma (Danny) has done a great job in writing this book; he has pointed out key issues in his book which must be read by teachers and pre-service teachers. I have known Diwakar since last five years, we both attended Niagara College, Canada for obtaining TESL Certification. Sharma has been one of the outstanding thinkers, I have met and have remained in touch with each other.

While teachers certainly need to understand how to teach and to have basic skills such as classroom management, there is no actual evidence that lengthy preparation programs achieve these goals any better than talented teachers into the classroom. Education system of various countries requires change and we must work on making teacher training and training of the teacher trainer part and parcel of educational pedagogy. In North America getting a degree in education might be easy, but maintaining the right to teach is difficult, as it is directly related to the keeping teacher license intact.

In Asia, once the instructor gets his or her degree in education, he or she becomes eligible for teaching in the job market. Asian teachers need to learn from Western teachers and *vice-versa*. Learning as we know is a lifelong process, it is noticed that most teachers develop their classroom skills fairly early in their teaching careers. Teachers entering the profession may find their initial teaching efforts stressful, but with experience they do acquire a gamut of teaching strategies that they work on throughout their teaching. The particular application of strategies a teacher uses constitutes his or her "teaching style". A teacher's style of teaching provides a means of coping with many of the routine demands of teaching, there is also a danger that it can hinder a teacher's professional growth.

We need to crosscheck our records and see how can teachers move beyond level of automatic responses to classroom situations and achieve a higher level of awareness of how they teach, and of the value and consequences of instructional decisions. In various parts of the world, where teachers are given due recognition to their contribution back to the society, recording of lessons is done on casual basis. For many aspects of teaching, audio or video recording of lessons can also provide a basis for reflection. While there are many useful insights to be gained from diaries and self-reports, they cannot capture the moment to moment processes of teaching. Many things happen simultaneously in a classroom, and some aspects of a lesson cannot be recalled.

Many significant classroom events may not have been observed by the teacher, let alone remembered, hence the need to supplement diaries or self-reports with recordings of actual lessons. Diwakar has included various aspects and factors important in delivering effective teaching methodologies and instructional strategies. While using some of the teaching strategies, the instructor remains active and the learners are passive audience this is very essential concept which must be understood by each and every instructor, teacher, teacher trainer and principles in education sectors. I have read the previous books written by Diwakar and I think he has been conducting research which is beneficial for the academicians and commoners in general. His book Teaching English as a Second Language is read around the world and is being quoted by various researchers around the world for conducting further studies.

I sincerely wish Diwakar, good luck in all of his future endeavors and would like him to continue writing, so that we can get some new food for thought and keep enhancing our knowledge.

EUNGTAE LEE
Senior Educationist
Gimhae Foreign Language High School
Gimhae City, South Korea

Preface

Education is required by all and must be given to all. Human kind needs knowledge and knowledge is transferred from one person to another. Indian history has given us numerous teachers in the past and most of these ordinary teachers have transformed themselves into extraordinary individuals. Becoming a teacher by virtue of getting a degree in teacher education is extremely easy but honing individual skills and getting accepted by the students in class is something which might not come easily to majority of teachers.

Many individuals enter the teaching stream with a master degree in a specialized subject and try to teach young learners, who not in every situation accept the teacher as a real mentor. Many experienced teachers often ask themselves the question, 'Am I ready to teach?' and very often well qualified teachers ask themselves the question, 'Am I ready to be a teacher trainer?' This has happened with me, when my boss wanted to run a workshop for teacher training. Each individual needs to answer the question for them of course. After having worked in Canada, China and now in India, I have had the opportunity of meeting various extraordinary teachers and not so well read teachers due to which sometimes I become hyper critical of teachers and teacher trainers. It seems to me that in any kind of teaching, the instructor needs the following:

- Excellent classroom management skills.
- A good understanding of the content you intend to

teach and an ability to transform it into (a) clear, succinct messages and practice via tasks and materials.
- Capacity and capability to engage participants, relate to them both one to one and in groups, and find out what they know and what they keenly want to know.
- Extraordinary classroom skills—for example, the ability to hold attention, question, wait, listen well, make good quality interventions, explain, demonstrate, negotiate learning that is interesting, meaningful and relevant for participants, monitor group work and synthesize everyone's offerings.

If you teach teenagers and intend to work with adults, you need to get some practice in working with adults. Adults may differ from young learners in their relaxed pace, longer concentration spans, constructive sense of humor, ability and willingness to bring in their longer life experience. As we already know that learning is the process through which we receive and process sensory data, encode such data as memories within the neural structures of our brain, and retrieve those memories of subsequent use.

Expert teacher trainers must enhance experience in all spheres of academics and must know how to handle different class sizes, types of students, types of courses, materials, teaching context, and so on. Many teacher trainers, mentors, educators, no matter how different work environments they belong to, find they are all deeply involved with certain core tasks such as helping teachers with lesson planning; observing teachers at work; giving feedback on observed lessons; and supporting teachers while they process new knowledge and experience different ways of teaching methodologies.

Unfortunately various teacher trainers, principals of B.Ed. and M.Ed. programs haven't been able to provide real teaching skills in the students. These principals are responsible for the poor state of affairs of Indian education system, which generates teachers who have no vision, no mission and literally no skills at all for grooming the younger generation. In various universities undue importance to the preparation of files, models is given and this gives absolute power in the hands of these principals, who abuse the system and do what they like and propagate what they feel worthwhile and suppress use of creativity. In India our education system is merely spreading information, that too in a distorted manner and due to this we are churning out parrots with various degrees, but little knowledge. Our present *Prime Minister Dr. Manmohan Singh* and *HRD Minister Kapil Sibal* have been talking about bringing out transforming change in the Indian educations system and economy at large, but very less has been done. We have been hearing a lot but we have been waiting to see real change in the Indian education system, we don't want to have teachers who do have degrees but no skills or bare minimum skills related to quality teaching. We don't need people with copied, fake and bogus doctorate degrees, instead we need instructors with willingness to bring change in the society.

This book has been written after going through tremendous mental dilemma as I have been involved with education and transforming knowledge, recruitment of faculty members, promotion and retrenchment of faculty members for various education groups based in India and Canada. Here in India the situation has been very severe in private as well as government colleges. Private sector students suffer because of very few quality instructors, who also keep hopping jobs for better financial prospects, whereas in government sector the system is jeopardized due to recruitment under quota systems.

Few skills—such as using tact, providing support and giving data-based commentary can transfer from language classroom to the teacher training classroom. Nevertheless, the core tasks of language teaching are pretty distinct in some ways and so their content and process, their what and how, need to be learned and practiced.

Many of the teacher trainers I know got into the field this way, and a good proportion of them did so by getting a job in teaching at the same school where they got their own initial training. In house faculty development programs (FDP), are pretty compelling for academic institutions for overall success in the academic stream. It is the responsibility of each and every well learned and groomed instructor to help in the training of other teachers in the academic organization. Even someone who has just a little more knowledge or experience than another can be helpful to the other, for a time. So even if you've just been teaching for one year, you can still be useful to the newly qualified teacher who's just arrived in your staffroom. The real teacher trainer is someone or we should say anyone who helps a colleague with an idea for their next lesson or who spends time listening to an upset colleague after a bad class. Lord Krishna has taught us a lot and his preachings have always been useful for strengthening the moral character of teachers and all other community leaders. What we have undergone Krishna knows, what Krishna has undergone, none of us know!

He had been a fish!
He had been a tortoise!
He had been a boar!
He had been a lion!
He had been a man bound with anger and vengeance, as Parasurama!
He had been the Perfect Man, as Lord Rama!
He not only knows how it is to be a man. He also knows, how it is to be a woman!
He has subjected himself to pregnancy and has given birth to Swami Iyyappa!
He knows the pain and joy of being a mother!
If you are a teenager, fallen in love, you can look unto him. Radhe Shyam, knows how you feel!
If you are a lover who is separated from your beloved, Sita Ram knows your longing!
If you are dealing with your enemies, you can look unto him for strategies!
If you are an artist, you can look unto him for nuances!
He knows, how it is to worship. He knows how it is to be worshipped.
He is a musician, a warrior, a philosopher, a ruler, a political strategist, a mystic, a cow herd and a charioteer.
What is in Krishna, you can find anywhere else.
But what is not in Krishna, you can't find anywhere else.
The Holy Gita is about transcending,
from the limited to the unlimited!
From transitory to the eternal!
From bondage to freedom!

We are ordinary humans. We are bound by hunger, thirst,
love, hate, anger, agreeability, pain, pleasure,
desire, aversion and much more.

Through this book, I have tried to highlight issues of extreme importance related to teachers and teacher training. I hope, after reading this book, you'll develop deep understanding of teacher training.

DIWAKAR SHARMA

Teaching : What and How?

In the years to come, instructors of colleges and adult learners will be faced with many challenges that did not previously exist. Compared to the classroom of former years, the evolution of the modern classroom has caused significant changes. The influx of multicultural and multilingual learners, the impact of technology, and the admission of learners with differing academic backgrounds have demanded the attention of educators everywhere. The changing economic and political presses throughout the world have impacted education and, us as the instructor.

You will feel the impact whether you teach in a continuing education program for business/ industry; in a liberal arts college with time honored traditions

"My subject and verb have agreed to disagree."

and values; in a community college with an open door policy; in a public research university with undergraduate as well as postgraduate programs; or in Language Instruction for New Comer's (LINC) situation {Applicable in Canada}. The learners of today and future will be highly motivated, more challenging and in many ways more enjoyable to teach.

With the concern for accountability and the realization that there are established strategies and techniques for instruction, there is greater emphasis upon quality instruction. Adult learners employed in business and industries expect a planned and organized classroom. It is no longer a question of whether there are going to be instructional objectives and strategies for teaching; it is question of how skilled instructions are in developing and delivering them.

One of the most important factors, however, remains the human elements of teaching. If you enjoy being a instructor, there is nothing wrong in telling the learners that you are there because you enjoy teaching. Being cheerful, open and understanding is always an asset to good teaching. Learners will like to hear your experiential anecdotes-share them. Look upon the class as project adult learners expect planning and preparation will not rebel if it is required. Be aware of your cultural and intellectual environment. Strive to be a good instructor and your teaching experiences will be exciting, rewarding and satisfying.

There may be learners who question why someone with your expertise would spend their time teaching a college course. Be prepared and have a few answers ready if learners ask. If they don't ask, you might want to include in your personal introduction. You certainly have good reasons. It might be to your advantage to communicate them. You may just enjoy teaching, like interaction with others, like the stimulation, enjoy being in front of a group, or feel it improves your own skills.

You should also give thought to your role in your academic environment. We need to know all parts of teaching fraternity; in short "what is an adjunct/part time instructor?" Adjunct faculties in recent years have assumed a greater responsibility to the educational mission of their colleges, institutions and universities. Many institutions depend upon part time faculty for fifty percent or more of credit hours of instruction taught.

Also in many institutions adjunct and part-time faculty serve on committees and accept other non-instructional assignments. Finally, adjunct faculties often teach in specialized areas where specific qualifications and expertise are needed. Wherever you are a continuing adjunct or a last-minute part time-replacement, yours is an important role and necessary to the integrity and success of your institution.

In your role as an adjunct/part time instructor, you will realize many of the intrinsic rewards of the profession. You are repaying your profession for its contribution to your own personal and professional development. There is satisfaction in providing service to your community and you will find that teaching builds self-esteem, offers personal rewards, and keeps you intellectually alive. Teaching can provide intellectual growth, community recognition and respect, and development of new professional contacts.

TEACHING METHODS

"Teaching should have little touch of magic and it should involve entertainment."

Overview

This presents a variety of teaching methodologies.

Learning Outcomes

At the completion of this section, instructors will understand:

(1) Discussed how to use different methods for different materials.
(2) Listed advantages and disadvantages of different methods.
(3) Related certain methods to teaching/learning/learning styles.

The teaching methods discussed here are as following:

(1) Lecture method

(2) Questioning techniques
(3) Demonstrations
(4) Small group work
(5) Case studies
(6) Role Playing

I. The Lecture Method

The lecture method is the most widely used and abused method of teaching and is one of the most popular methods in Indian context. The lecture method is the most necessary ingredient to all teaching methods as it is component part of most other methods.

"I expect you all to be independent, innovative, critical thinkers who will do exactly as I say!"

Advantages of Lecturing

- ❖ Permits dissemination of unpublished or not readily available material
- ❖ Allows the instructor to precisely determine the aims, content, organization, pace and direction of a presentation
- ❖ Can be used to arouse interest in a subject
- ❖ Can complement and clarify text material
- ❖ Facilitates large class communication
- ❖ Can motivate learners

Limitations

1. Lecture is a one channel method. In this, presentation is emphasized, while the learners function as passive listeners. This creates dullness in the class-room as interaction between the learner and the instructor ceases to occur.
2. Learners get a few chances for responding. They get no Motivation for acquiring knowledge.
3. As the matching material gets more complicated, the learners start feeling boredom.

Objectives

1. To achieve the lowest objective of the cognitive aspect.
2. To achieve the highest objective of the cognitive aspect.
3. To achieve the affective objectives.
4. As the main teaching aspects are not included in the lecture method carefully therefore, most of the instructors usually remain unsuccessful in achieving these objectives.

Suggestions for Success

1. As lecture is an art a continuous effort is needed in order to gain success in it.
2. The person delivering lecture should know the subject fully.
3. The contents of the lecture should be organized systematically according to the interest and mental level of the learners.
4. Any easy language and meaningful and interesting illustration should be used in lecturing.
5. An appropriate teaching material should be used while lecturing.
6. An effort should be made to avoid irrelevant references and to establish contact between one topic and the other.
7. The lecture should be interesting. Books or the notes should not be used while delivering a lecture.
8. Important points should be emphasized during lecturing.
9. The lecture should not be so lengthy and formal as the learners start feeling boredom.
10. The lecture should follow an interaction between the instructor and the learners.

2. The Questioning Techniques

Have you ever considered how much of your teaching time is spent in asking questions or why questioning is such a widely used technique? The art of good questioning is developed by practice and we all have to work smartly for achieving expertise in this technique. Skill in this art permits the instructor to be much more effective and efficient in teaching/learning process.

Questions can be used to:

- ❖ Arouse curiosity, thereby motivating further interest
- ❖ Encourage the participation of learner
- ❖ Help learners determine their own progress
- ❖ Help the instructor determine learner progress

A good question should have the following characteristics:

- ❖ Concise, including only one idea
- ❖ Short enough for learners to remember
- ❖ Timely, interesting, thought-provoking, and relevant to the lesson being taught
- ❖ Stated to stress the key points of a major lesson topic
- ❖ Stated to require more that a guessing response
- ❖ Stated in such a way that it does not suggest the answer

3. Demonstrations

The demonstration method of teaching such skills is a most effective way of exposing learners to the manipulative process being examined. Ideally, after the demonstrations, the learner should be able to imitate/practice the process.

Demonstrations have an important role to play in the teaching of concepts and principles. A well-organized demonstration can effectively explain to learners why something works the way it does.

4. Small Group Work

Group work is an effective teaching methodology to present, discuss, and evaluate course curriculum. The instructor's role is important in the preparation, instruction, and monitoring of group activities in the classroom.

Group Work

- ❖ Encourage learner participation
- ❖ Builds learner's confidence

- Can allow for self-evaluation to monitor understand or progress

5. The Case Study Method

The case study method simulates true-to-life situations. It provides a tool for applying theory to practical problems. It is used best when learning outcomes call for learner to transfer information to new situations, make decisions, problem-solve, or demonstrate independent thinking.

Advantages of the Case Study Method

- Encourages learners to think logically, analytically, and constructively
- Enhances critical thinking and practical judgment
- Requires learners to translate ideas and concepts into practical action plans
- Force learners to develop ideas and to articulate them clearly

6. Role Playing

Role-playing is an "acting out" of a situation, problem, or topic of concern. In role-playing the players attempt to make a situation clear to themselves and to the audience by playing the roles of participation in the situation.

Benefits of Role-Playing

Role-playing is an important technique that requires to use properly so as not to reduce harmful effects instead of the desired outcomes. When properly used, role-playing can:

- ✓ Stimulate interest and participation in class,
- ✓ Give insight into the roles a person plays in real life,
- ✓ Teach learners to perform new roles and adjust to the group they are in, and
- ✓ Help develop clever communication.

ESTABLISHING A TEACHING ENVIRONMENT

Over the past two decades, there has been a major

movement in higher education called "the learning college" movement or community-centered learning. Quite simply, this means that learning has become learner-centered rather than instructor-centered. This is especially important to adjunct faculty members, most of who come from the surrounding community and thus are aware of community customs.

When establishing a learner-centered learning environment, one should first examine the instructor–learner relationship. The simple and obvious way to develop a relationship with your learners is be yourself and be honest, establishing communication in the classroom the same as you would in any other human endeavor. There are, however additional specific steps that can be taken to establish a proper learning environment. The four areas in which the learning environment should: instructor expectations, teaching behavior, physical space, and strategies for creating an environment for learning (Helen Burnstad, 2000). It would be impossible to describe these areas completely but some of Burnstad's major points are mentioned below:

- *Instructor expectations*: The expectations that you as an instructor have of yourself may differ considerably from those of the learners in your class. This does not mean that you need to change your style. However, you need to examine the expectations of your learners in terms of their position on issues and principles that may arise in class.
- *Instructor behaviors*: It is important that you examine your presence in the classroom. Learners will sense whether you really love your subject matter or are teaching the course to reach some unrelated professional goal. A pleasant personality is important. Enthusiasm may be demonstrated through energy and engaging in activities with learners. Remember, your feelings concerning the expectations of your learners will unwittingly be reflected in the success or failure of your learners.

- *Physical space*: Although in most cases you will have little control over the physical aspects of the classroom environment, there are several things that can be done by the instructor. If possible, you may physically move seats so that dialogue and eye contact are easier. The concept of physical space should be interpreted taking in consideration the place, city, province, state or country in mind. You should monitor the attention span of your learners; sense the need for reinforcement; calculate the time-on-task; and encourage learners to move, interact and ask questions.
- *Environmental strategies*: Different instructors follow different strategies, some strategies that can improve the classroom environment include:
  1. Introducing yourself to your learners with some personal anecdotes.
  2. Being prepared for learners with diverse backgrounds.
  3. Using an activity for getting to know your learners whether a game, a writing assignment, or reference card, etc.
  4. Learning each learner's name and providing ways for learners to get to know one another.
  5. Preparing a complete and lively syllabus. You can have your learners from a previous class leave a legacy by asking them to write a letter for incoming learners, then sharing it.

Whether one is establishing a classroom environment or doing day-to-day activities, it is important that you be as positive in your learner-instructor relationship as toward your subject matter. Make yourself available for learner contact, either physically or electronically. You must try to take personal interest in each learner and never judge or stereotype learners. If you are or you want to be seen as a well read instructor it would be in your benefit to work according to the lesson plan prepared by you.

SAMPLE A

UNIT Preliminary, identifying information could include course number and name, unit and lesson titles, section number, date and time, instructor's name, etc.

Lesson Topic

Learning Outcomes: These learning outcomes should be stated in terms of the learner, not the instructor. You do not state what you will do. You state what learners will be able to do as a result of instruction given by you.

Introduction: Orient the learners to:

1. What the learning outcomes of the lessons are,
2. How the lesson is related to them,
3. How it links to preceding and future classroom activities, and
4. What will be expected of them?

Gain the attention of the learners and motivate them sufficiently to hold their attention. Outline your introduction and record the amount of time to be allotted to it.

Method: Select the most appropriate technique or method with which to communicate the material to the learners, and select the most appropriate learning experiences by which the learners can apply the material. Ensure that learning activities match your outcomes.

Learning Activity: Briefly describe each learning activity. List the activities in the sequence you plan to follow. Attach time frames to each learning experience.

Resources: List all of the resources, materials and aids required for this lesson.

Evaluation: Use the summary to:

1. Pull loose ends together
2. Draw conclusions
3. Evolve generalizations
4. Reiterate major concepts.

Reinforce for learners where they were headed, where they have been, where they should be now and why, and where they will go from here. List your summary points and attach a time to this section.

SAMPLE B

TIME

PRELIMINARY INFORMATION
WHAT
WHOM
WHEN
WHO
WHERE

LEARNING OUTCOMES

INTRODUCTION

Motivators:

Links:

Outline:

Content

TEACHING METHODS
1.
2.
3.
4.
5.
6.
7.
8.
9.
10.

SUMMARY AND EVALUATION

RESOURCES

ANALYSIS OF LESSON PLAN

It is advisable to analyze your lesson plan, using the points in the checklist that follows as a guide:

- Does the Introduction:

    (a) Tie this lesson in with pervious lessons or previous trainee experience;
    (b) Provide for review where desirable;
    (c) Show the value of learning this material;
    (d) Arouse interest;
    (e) Contain a clear, precise aim for the lesson;
    (f) Give an outline, where desirable?

- Does the Presentation:

    (a) Provide new material arranged in logical order;
    (b) Develop from the known to the unknown, and from simple to complex;
    (c) Make connections between bits of learning;
    (d) Supply an outline for demonstrations and performance, if any;
    (e) Include examples, illustrations, and devices for clarification of difficult areas;
    (f) Integrate this information with other training, where possible;
    (g) Give directions for use of aids;
    (h) Include sketches for whiteboard work, if board is to used;
    (i) Ask key questions and elicit desired answers?

- Does the Application:

    (a) Provide for trainee practice;
    (b) Contain pre-arranged questions;
    (c) Relate this lesson to those that follow;
    (d) Summarize important points and state conclusions reached?

LESSON PLAN

INRODUCTION

Preliminaries

- What,Why,Where (suitable order)
- Lesson Approach
- Pre-Test (if necessary)

BODY

Stage I

- Brief Introduction
- Present Teaching Points—Knowledge
- Present Steps—Skill
- Any Questions Stage I
- Confirm Stage I

Stage II

- Same as Stage I
- Any Questions Stage II
- Confirm Stage II

Add as many stages as necessary to cover material

- Short Summary of Entire Lesson
- Any Questions on Entire Lesson

TEST

- Formal or informal
- Give instruction
- Conduct
- Correct
- Clear up weak areas

CONCLUSION

- Summary of entire lesson
- Remotivate
- Other handouts (if necessary)
- What to expect next lesson
- Closing Statement

CHECK LIST FOR ANALYZING A LESSON PLAN

A. In the PREAMBLE have you included:
- Topic and length of lesson?
- List of tools, equipment and aids?
- References?
- Statement of aim and lesson objectives?

B. Does the INRODUCTION:
- Tie this lesson in with previous lesson(s) or previous learner experience?
- Provide for review when desirable?
- Show value of learning this material?
- Arouse interest?
- Contain a clear, precise aim for the lesson?
- Give the outline?

C. Does the PRESENTATION provide:
- New material arranged in logical order?
- For recaps, between pockets?
- For development from known to unknown; from simple to complex?
- Complete outline for demonstrations and performance, if any?
- Directions for use of aids?
- Sketches for the blackboard work, if board is to be used?

D. Does the APPLICATION:
- Provide for learner practice?
- Contain pre-arranged Questions?
- Link this lesson with (one's) follow?

E. Is the PLAN:
- Screened so that all material points towards the objectives?
- In a form that makes it usable during class period?
- Practical with regard to time-material relationships?

* For your reference, sample lesson plan is included here and you should try to craft your lesson plan similar to the one provided to you.

CHARACTERISTICS OF GOOD TEACHING

Using one's mind in the pursuit of knowledge and at the same time sharing it with others is very gratifying. The responsibility for a class and the potential influence on learners can be stimulating. It remains stimulating however, only so long as the instructor continues to grow and remains dynamic.

The qualities of good teaching are quite simple:

- Know your subject.
- Know and like your learners.
- Understand your culture.
- Possess professional teaching skills and strategies.
- Know how to appreciate others.
- Know how to avoid being judgmental.

Knowing your subject means simply that you have a command of your discipline and the capability of calling upon resources. Knowing learners is part of the teaching process and is aided by formal and informal communication within and outside the classroom. Understanding our cultural milieu has become increasingly complex for today's instructor. Sensitivity to the diverse cultures in your classroom is necessary to succeed in teaching.

Exercise for the First Day of Class

Climate Setting Introduction Exercise

Goals: 1. To help people meet and learn a few things about each other.

Goals: 2. To create a spirit of friendliness and get rid of the tension that is present at the beginning of a new group.

Goals: 3. To develop a "Learning community" in the classroom.

Group Size: 7-12 people.

Time Required: At least 30 minutes.

Equipment: Flipchart paper and felt-tipped markers.

Directions: Give each participant a piece of flipchart paper and a felt-tipped marker. The facilitator then gives the instruction to the participants to divide their paper into quadrants, titling each space as follows:

1. Name (What you want to be called).
2. Life History (Describe in pictures or words).
3. Hobbies.
4. Goals for today/Goals for the future.

Instruct the participants that in the next fifteen minutes they are to fill out the required information on their flipchart paper. This is followed by the participants taking turns sharing their information with the entire group.

METHODOLOGY OF TEACHING AND INSTRUCTIONAL STRATEGIES

Development of Methodology

The actual origin of latest terms of modern methodology could be traced to 'great Didactic' of Johann Amos Comenius who lived in the seventeenth century. Comenius believed that all instructions should be carefully graded and arranged in an order which appears to be natural. The instructor/instructor in his/her preaching of methods should appeal to make sense and must be acceptable to the understanding and perception of a child. All outstanding discoveries and revolutionary ideas are opposed and are somehow categorized as controversial and even termed bigotry, the same happened with the work of Comenius and all the research work was buried as it was against the religious beliefs.

In the second half of the eighteenth century Emile of Rousseau laid the deep foundations of new methodologies. Rousseau's work was inspirational/motivational for forward looking and progressive educators. As a progressive forward looking educator Rousseau improved and reinvented his ideas. In the core of his work Rousseau, started with the notion that everything is good as it comes from the hands of the creator of nature; but everything degenerates in hands of man. It is well accepted fact that we can see three great instructors : nature, man and things.

Psychology also came into action, with Johann Heinrich Pestalozzi who attempted to psychologically hypnotize instruction. Pestalozzi declared that education in itself was not constructive as it was drawing out process instead of a pouring in process. He Pestalozzi was rather convinced that the root of growth and development laid in the nature of the child and the way of instruction must be sought and constructed towards achieving that particular end. With the change of time and thought process two disciples of Pestalozzi, Willhelm August Froebel and Johann Frederich Herbart worked on the art of developing elaborate systems of education.

Froebel's work dealt largely with the Kindergrarten/ infancy stage. Herbart gave his famous Herbartian steps which cast a flood of light on creating methods, which existed and which were related with the existence of methodological development. His steps injected stimulus relief which brought various motional movements in the field of education. Herbert condemned the typical rote method and stressed comprehension and association. He forcefully mentioned that the outcome of education was not the strengthening of mental faculties but rather was associated with development of ideas which were appreciative but revolutionary to an extreme extend. It was observed that education under stress resulted in mental agony and was not strengthening of the mental faculties but rather the building up of an appreciative mass of ideas was innovative. His theories became popular in Germany between 1865 and 1885. His ideas travelled from Germany to US and received universal acceptance.

The recognition of Herbartian influence was a transitional one and it prepared the way for newer and better concepts of education by 1910. Herbartian system of education was criticized because it stressed the instructor and formal procedure of teaching; the new theories of educational philosophy emphasized on the learner. Individual attention in the classroom is a must, but not at the cost of group work or socialization of individual. Almost all innovative methods and procedures were included in the research work and were used to promote different aspects of learning.

Socialization can be used in connection with individual development. Socialization is necessary in social studies, even more than any other subject in the school. The pupil can learn and develop through his own activities intermingled with the activities of the group. Education must begin with the child, it must be adopted to the needs and requirements of the child as he grows. Only in this manner, can the individual be made socially efficient.

NATURE OF METHODOLOGY

1. The choice of a suitable method by a instructor depends upon many factors such as the learner, the nature of the subject and the topic; the facilities available and above all the attitude of the instructor. There is no single road to successful teaching as Dr. R. Vajreshwari puts it: There are many roads, highways and by-ways, royal roads and narrow lanes, delightful paths and rugged and rough ones, functional and decorative and all these help in reaching the ultimate goal of spreading the key word and wisdom of knowledge.
2. As the method of teaching arises out of the need of a learning situation, so it cannot be the same for all times and all situations, nor can it be the same for all instructors and all subjects.
3. As an instrument a method should play the role of a willing servant rather than of a tyrannical master.
5. By and large all methods are interconnected.
6. A method is not a mechanical device for passing on facts and figures. It should create the right reaction and response and improve the values of learning and foster right attitudes.

Use of Methodology

Indian Education Commission said, "it has to be remembered that advances in classroom practice never occur on a broad front, with all the instructors and the schools moving forward in unison. . . . But the work of the best instructors can be crippled, if they are not permitted, encouraged and helped to go beyond the departmental prescriptions". The success of an educational reform will depend upon the flexible approach where the good school or the good instructor is able to go ahead and the necessary supports are provided to the weaker institutions to introduce the reform gradually.

The Commission further observed, "In a modern society where the rate of change and growth of knowledge is very rapid, the educational system must be elastic and dynamic. It must give freedom to its basic units, the individual learner in a school, the individual instructor among his colleagues and the individual school (cluster of schools) within the system to move in a direction or at a pace which is different from that of similar other units within the system without being unduly hampered by the structure of the system as a whole. In this process the freedom offered to the instructor is the most vital, it is almost synonymous with the freedom of the school for the learners can rarely be freer than the men and women who teach them.

Characteristics of Good Methodology

1. It should aim at inculcating 'love of work' and 'love for work'.
2. It should aim at developing the desire to do work with the highest measure of efficiency of which one is capable. The academic administrative motive of every school and its learners should be "Everything that is worth doing at all is worth doing well"—whether it be making a speech, writing a composition, drawing a map, cleaning the classroom, making a book rack, developing any research publication, organizing any function or forming a queue.
3. It should provide numerous opportunities of participation in freely accepted projects and activities in which discipline and cooperation are constantly in demand.
4. It should aim at developing the capacity for "crystal clear logical thinking" which distinguishes every truly educated proactive individual. Whether a learner is

asked to make a speech in a debating society or to write an essay or to answer a question in philosophy, business, or science or to perform an experiment, the accent should always be on clear thinking and on lucid expression which is a mirror of clear thought.

5. It should expand the range of learners' interest. We would urge all schools to provide in the time-table, at least one free period every day in which learners may pursue their favourite hobbies and creative activities individually or in groups, preferably under the guidance of some interested instructor, Indian. Education Commission said.
6. It should aim at providing opportunities to learners to apply practically the knowledge that has been acquired by them.
7. It should aim at transforming present bookish schools into work schools or activity schools.
8. It should train the learners in the art of study and the use of reference material such as the list of contents and index in books, the dictionary, and reference books like the encyclopedia.
9. It should be adapted to suit different levels of intelligence.
10. It should be such as to balance the claims of individual work with, cooperative or group effort. The training of emotions, attitudes and social capacities take place best in the context of projects and units of work undertaken cooperatively. The Secondary Education Commission has recommended that the instructors should be so trained that they are able to visualize and organize at least a part of the curriculum in the form of projects and activity-units which groups of learners may take up and carry to completion.

Seven-fold Division of Methodology

- *Inspirational methods*: These are primarily based on high activity on the part of the instructor. Giving a sermon to the learners or to any group of learners is a good example of this methodology.

- *Expository methods*: In these cognitive emphasis is very high, while learner activity and emphasis on experience is low. One good example of expository method is the lecture method in which the main emphasis is on imparting cognitive information to the learners.
- *Natural learning methods*: The main rationale of these methods is that learning takes place in a natural way and planning for learning is not necessary. Learners are left on their own, with free and unplanned activity. Thus, the emphasis on learning activity is high, whereas it is low on planned experience and on cognitive inputs.
- *Individualized methods*: These are well known mainly through the popularity of programmed instruction. Their main characteristic is the guided search/research encouraged by the instructor. In programmed instruction, self-study, computer-oriented instruction, case method, and prescribed experiments in science are examples of individualized learning emphasizing that each learner should learn at his own pace.
- *Encounter methods*: Carl Rogers popularized the term 'encounter', although several other terms are used like T-Group, sensitivity training, interpersonal confrontation and so on. In these methods the main emphasis is on experience and learner activity on providing experience through confrontation or through encounter, and not through cognitive understanding. These methods are affective in change in basic behavioral patterns and developing new ways of looking at things.
- *Discovery methods*: These are high on all the three dimensions learner activity, experience and experimentation by the learner, and cognitive understanding. Simulations primarily come under the category as also self-generated experiments in science. The main emphasis of methods is on problem-solving and providing necessary framework to the learner, so

that while solving the problem the learner is also able to learn the rationale, and logic of what he has done.

DEFINITION OF TEACHING STRATEGY

According to Smith, "The term strategy refers to pattern of acts that serve to attain certain outcomes and to guard against certain others. It is clear that word strategy means the determination of some policy by planning before presenting the contents with the help of which the learner's force is faced and the teaching objectives are achieved. In this way, the pre-planning of the lesson is key to success. Hence, every instructor should be skilled in this part of pre-Planning.

Stones Morris moved a bit further and said, "Teaching strategy is a generalized plan for a lesson which includes structure, desired learner behaviour in terms of goals, instruction and an outline of planned tactics necessary to implement the strategy. The teaching strategies are more comprehensive than the teaching methods; the teaching methods include only presentation of contents. Contrary to this, teaching strategy includes all the aspects like contents, task analysis, teaching objectives, the expected changes in the behaviour of the learners, their interest, attitudes, capacities, abilities, needs, mental level and human behaviour, etc.

After having worked in different academic environments, it sometimes gets difficult for me to accept the teaching methodologies which are being used by various instructors at different levels of imparting education. Becoming a instructor or instructor trainer is extremely easy in India and it is being observed that many of the instructors the moment they get the bachelor degree in Education or the master degree in Education, tend to stop being members of the learning fraternity. The course curricula of B.Ed as well as M.Ed is outdated and non-productive, most of the learners trying to get B.Ed/M.Ed degree through even the leading Universities of India inclusive of DU/ GGSIPU hardly learn how to teach. Affiliated institutes don't have qualified faculty members and even Principals are seldom accustomed to the real life teaching. Practical aspect of teaching is missing as most of the work done by the learners in the B.Ed/ M.Ed programme is not up to the demand of the industry. Stress is given on obtaining good grades and most of the instructors in the making are pressurized to do as per the taste of the Principals running the programme. Education is extremely important and the instructor must be knowledgeable enough to give learners what they really want and what would really help learners in becoming informed citizens and valuable contributors in the society.

Education scenario in India is changing and we the educators want to see major change in the teaching style of faculty members involved in the education of B.Ed/M.Ed programmes. Teaching should not be restricted to the theoretical knowledge, but should emphasize on practical use of the techniques which would enhance the level of knowledge required for a well groomed and informed individual. We in India need a new system of education, through which we can develop leaders, not followers. Flattery and show-off need to go and all these bad traits should be replaced with dignity, sincerity and desire of upbringing instructor educators who'll infuse change and motivate learners to lead the nation ahead.

TYPES OF INSTRUCTIONAL STRATEGIES

The instructional strategies are used for achieving the teaching goals. While using some of the teaching strategies, the instructor remains active and the learners are passive audience. It results in the non-development of all the potentialities of the learners. Such a situation needs some change in this instructor centered/instructor talk time/teaching strategy so that more and more learning experiences learners may gain and the teaching objectives may be achieved conveniently by bringing desired change in their behaviour's. The teaching strategies are divided into two categories keeping in view the class-room management, situation, and the instructor's attitude:

- Autocratic strategies.
- Democratic strategies.

1. *Autocratic Strategies* : Autocratic strategies are traditional teaching strategies. These are content centres and instructor-centered. While using these

strategies, the instructors place is primary and the learners is secondary. The instructor determines the content himself, by considering himself an ideal and by suppressing learner's interests, attitudes, capacities, abilities and needs. He tries to impose knowledge forcibly from outside in the minds of the learners. While using such teaching strategies, an instructor with narrow attitude may be active, but all the learners of his class remain passive audience out of fear and they go on obeying his instructions in spite of incorrect instructions. In such a situation, they don't have any freedom for their expression. Hence, only mental development is emphasized in these autocratic strategies, group development is not cared for at all for achieving cognitive objectives. Autocratic teaching strategies include: (1) Lecture, (2) Demonstration, (3) Theoretical study, (4) Programmed Instruction, etc. This style of teaching is very much prevalent in India as well as most of the Asian Countries, which are not yet exposed to the North American style of education. If the North American style of education and especially the style of education which is used in Canada if adopted in India, majority of instructor trainers/ principals might be jobless as they are the ones who hardly want to change. Indian educators should realize the fact that India needs productive members of the society and that will come only with vocational education.

2. *Democratic Strategies*: Democratic strategies are learner centered. The learners determine themselves the contents. In the use of these strategies, the pupil's place is primary and that of instructors is secondary. Hence, maximum interaction occurs between the learners and the instructor. This develops their constructive capacitating accordance to the interests, attitudes, capacities, abilities, needs and mental level of the learners. Democratic strategies are objective. Hence, the genius learners like them gain maximum advantages. The main peculiarity of these strategies is that the maximum social development is possible

through these strategies. The following strategies are included in the democratic category strategies (1) Discussion, (2) Discovery, (3) Heurism, (4) Project, (5) Review, (6) Assignment, (7) Tutorial Group, (8) Brain Storming, (9) Role Playing, (10) Independent Study, and (11) Sensitivity, etc.

Learning by Doing

The principle of education 'Through work' or 'Learning by doing' has been accepted by all the progressive educators and in all the progressive countries of the world. All educationists recognize that activity is an important instrument of education. Following are some important views in this connection:

1. *Aristotle* : He pleaded that a proper understanding and appreciation of music comes only when the learner himself practices it.
2. *Comenius:* According to him, impression must be ensured by expansion and what has to be done must be learned by doing.
3. *Rousseau*: Rousseau protested against the traditional methods of teaching very vehemently and declared, children are first restless and then curious—Instead of making the child stick to his books, I keep him busy in workshop, his hands will work to the profit of his mind.
4. *Pestalozzi*: He called the traditional system as the worldly system of teaching. According to him, our unpsychological schools are essentially only artificial stifling machines for destroying all the results of the power and experience, the nature herself brings to life in them. After they have enjoyed sensuous life for five whole years, we make all nature round them vanish before their eyes; tyrannically stop the delightful course of their unrestricted freedom peg them up like sheep; pitilessly chain them for hours, days, weeks, months, years, to the contemplation of unnatural and unattractive letter.
5. *Froebel* : Play is the chief activity of childhood which he considers as the highest phase of child development—

for it is self-active representation of the inner-play is the purest, most spiritual activity of man at this stage. It gives, therefore, joy, freedom, contentment, inner and outer rest, peace with the world. It holds the source of all that is good. But without national conscious guidance, says Forebel, Childish activity degenerates into aimless play instead of preparing for these tasks of life for which it is designed.

6. *John Dewey*: According to him, the school is a special environment, where a certain quality of life and certain types of activities and occupations are provided with the object of securing child's development along desirable lines. Dewey endeavored to substitute bookish learning by experience. He strongly recommended investigation and experimentation. According to him, the school is a "special environment" where a certain quality of life and certain types of activities and occupations are provided with the object of securing learners' development along desirable lines. The instructor, according to him, is a guide and director, he steers the boat but the energy that propels it must come from those who are learning.
7. *Madam Montessori*: She shifted the emphasis from "teaching to learning". She believed that self-education is the best method by which the child learns in his own way and at his own rate. She used the word 'Directress'.
8. *M.K. Gandhi*: He said: Let us now try a halt and concentrate on education of the child properly through manual work, not as a side activity but as a prime means of intellectual training.

Thus, a long list of distinguished experts in education have advocated that knowledge can best be given through constructive activities suitable to the child.

Broader View of the Term 'Activity'

Activity does not mean mere physical activity. As Ryburn puts, Activity of the intelligence and also of the emotions, and of the will. If a learner is to develop all sides of his personality, then it is necessary for him to be active in all ways, to exercise all the different powers he has. Doing is necessary in learning. It is not a mere device but a part and parcel of the learning process without which learning is not complete. Doing must be with a purpose. Following are included in activities:

1. *Instinctive Tendencies*: Children are active by nature. Innovation and development transform into a powerful drive in childhood. The hands of the child are ever ready to make new things. If he does not find material to construct, he begins to destroy. In fact, construction and destruction are the aspects of the same activity. The instructor should utilize this instinct by encouraging children to construct and create things.
2. *Curiosity:*. Children want to understand the environment and put hundreds of questions to instructors, parents and friends. This urge must be exploited.
3. *Acquisition:* Children are fond of collecting things. They should be encouraged to collect useful things for their museum.
4. *Self-Motivation*: Motivation facilitates the process of learning by doing. It arouses the interest of the child and once interest is aroused, the child becomes active, attentive and learns by doing.
5. *Purposeful Activities*: Abstract things cannot be followed and understood by children. Mental activities should be followed by concrete activities and this gives them the idea what they are doing and that with some purpose and aim.
6. *Utilization of All Senses*: The children are required to utilize all of their senses in learning by doing. Children have to be attentive in learning, seeing, feeling, smelling and sometimes testing even. This makes learning fruitful.
7. *Close Relation of Mind and Body*: Mental activities fail to develop harmoniously without interaction of mind and body which are closely related. In learning by doing the hand and the head work in close co-operation and the learning becomes successful.

8. *Lessening of Fatigue*: Mental work is more fatigue-giving than the manual one and if children are kept busy in purely mental activities, they feel mental fatigue. But when we co-ordinate both mental and manual work, fatigue is lessened to a great extent.
9. *The Principle of Linking Learning with Life*: Learning is linked with the life and the environment of the child and thus it becomes part and parcel of our nature. In a lesson on gardening if we take the learners to a garden and explain to them the relevant topic, it creates more impression and the learners learn it easily.
10. *Social Development*: Social development is as important as individual development. Children want to work in groups. In learning by doing they learn from each other and thus develop qualities like, co-operation. Sometimes learning by doing takes the form of productive activities as is the case in basic education. The learners then produce things for society. Thus they develop feelings of being a part of the community and try to be useful for it.
11. *Use of All the Theories of Learning*: 'Learning by trial and error', 'learning by imitating' others and 'learning insight'—all are employed in learning by doing. Thus learning becomes quicker, easier and more effective.

Principles of Learning by Doing

The scope of learning by doing principle is not only related to the learning of various subjects but also to the out-of-class activities and most of the hands on training programs are based on learning by doing. Instructors must be smart and willing to change and learners should be engaged in debating, editing, scouting, dramatizing, etc. Games and sports are the other fields. A well trained individual takes all opportunities to render social service to community. Social education centres, social service clubs, peer tutoring arenas should be started. Recreational courses alongwith social support workers help in transforming the youth for contributing in the development of the society.

Selecting Appropriate Teaching Tactics

When teaching is organized the instructor should, at first, select appropriate teaching tactics or as we know acceptable teaching methodologies. Teaching tactics are more comprehensive than the teaching strategies. A teaching tactic can be used in many teaching strategies. By using one or more teaching tactics in one strategy, the contents can be made easy precise and understandable. The teaching tactics make the knowledge stable. Hence, for the qualitative progress of teaching, we use various tactics according to the conditions or learning structures. While the subject-matter is analyzed it is divided into sub-parts. After this, each sub-part is divided into various essential elements and these are arranged in a sequence.

TYPES OF LEARNING STRUCTURES AND TEACHING TACTICS

Each element of the subject-matter has its own structure. The instructor selects teaching strategies tactics and aids on the basis of the structure of each element of the subject-matter acts as the norm or a criterion in the selection of teaching strategy, tactic and aid. Hence, one can present the structure of each element of the subject-matter only by applying or using the teaching strategy. Hence, the instructor should keep in mind the learning structure while selecting the teaching tactic. In order to select appropriate teaching tactic the knowledge of learning structure is essential. Following are the types of learning structures and the tactics to be used in them:

1. Signal Learning Structure and Teaching Tactics.
2. Chain Learning Structure and Teaching Tactics.
3. Multiple Discrimination Learning Structure and Teaching Tactics.
4. Concept Learning Structure and Teaching Tactics.
5. Principle Learning Structure and Teaching Tactics.

Signal Learning Structure and Teaching Tactics

Signal Learning Structure is termed as stimulus-response because its basis is stimulus response. The learners respond to a special stimulus. They continuously carry on the practice while organizing the stimulus and the response. This consolidates the relationship of stimulus and response. The instructor should compel the learners to respond to the stimulus. Then they should be motivated to give correct answers. In the end, they should be put gradually to the exercise relating to the response through reinforcement. Thus, the following teaching tactics should be used in the signal learning structure:

1. Establishing Contiguity.
2. Constant Practice and Rehearsal.
3. Reinforcing the correct Response.

Chain Learning Structure and Teaching Tactics

The chain learning structure is the sequence of facts and symbols learnt earlier. The chain is sometimes formed from the verbal activities such as, poetic recitation and motor activities such as, cycling. This chain is of three types:

(i) Progressive Chain, (ii) Rote learning, and (iii) Retrogressive chain. In the progressive chain, starting from signals we reach upto the end of the chain. In the rote learning, the chain is acquired by cramming (Most of Asian learners follow the rote learning tactic, as this is often promoted by the instructors). In the retrogressive chain, we start from the last activity and then reach to the beginning of the chain. Out of these three tactics, retrogressive chain is more effective. (i) It functions as reinforcement, and (ii) It makes possible to acquire efficiency in the task.

Multi-Discrimination Learning Structure and Teaching Tactics

In multi-discrimination learning structure both the signals and chains are included. Facts are separated from each other and the comparisons are made clear. For this, learners should take care of two things. (i) stimulus and response should be clear, and (ii) all the things should be presented simultaneously. Learners should proceed from simple to complex, so that they may understand the difference. In this multi-discrimination learning structure, the instructor should use the following two tactics:

(i) Distinctive Conditions.
(ii) Simultaneous presentation.

Principle Learning Structure and Teaching Tactics

In the principle learning structure, a chain of two or more concepts is included. In this chain to know each principle, concepts relating to it should be clear to the learners. In order to provide knowledge of principle learning structure the instructors should try to let the learners recall the concepts and make a chain of these concepts. Hence, he should use the following two tactics in the principle learning structure:

(i) Recalling the concept.
(ii) Chaining the concepts.

Tutorial Method

As often heard in democracy, it is the fundamental right of every person to get education. Therefore, instead of individual teaching, group-teaching is emphasized in democracy so that the large group may be educated at the low rate of expenditure. In group teaching, an instructor cannot solve the 'personal problems of every learner. If he does this, he cannot finish his fixed syllabi in a time-bound manner. To remove this drawback of group-teaching, learners are divided into small groups so that their personal problems may be solved successfully. Tutorial is a sub-part of the class in which an instructor tries to solve the problems of the small groups of the learners through individual teaching types of Tutorials.

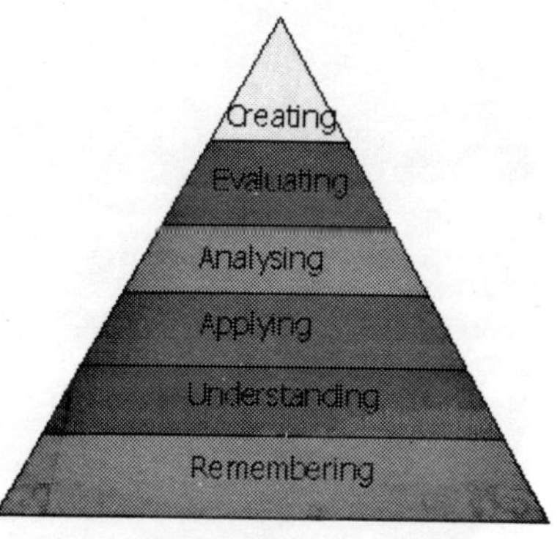

Types of Tutorials

1. *Supervised Tutorial*: In the supervised tutorials, the talented learners and the instructors discuss the

problems time to time. The learners put up their difficulties. Then the instructor tries to solve those problems.

2. *Group Tutorials*: These are conducted to solve the problem of the grown up learners of average level. They can be organized successfully only by an instructor who possesses adequate knowledge of Group Dynamics and Social Psychology.
3. *Practical Tutorials*: These are conducted to develop the physical skill and to achieve the objectives of psychomotor skill. Learners have to work in the laboratory. Such tutorials are more useful for younger and learners of lower-classes.

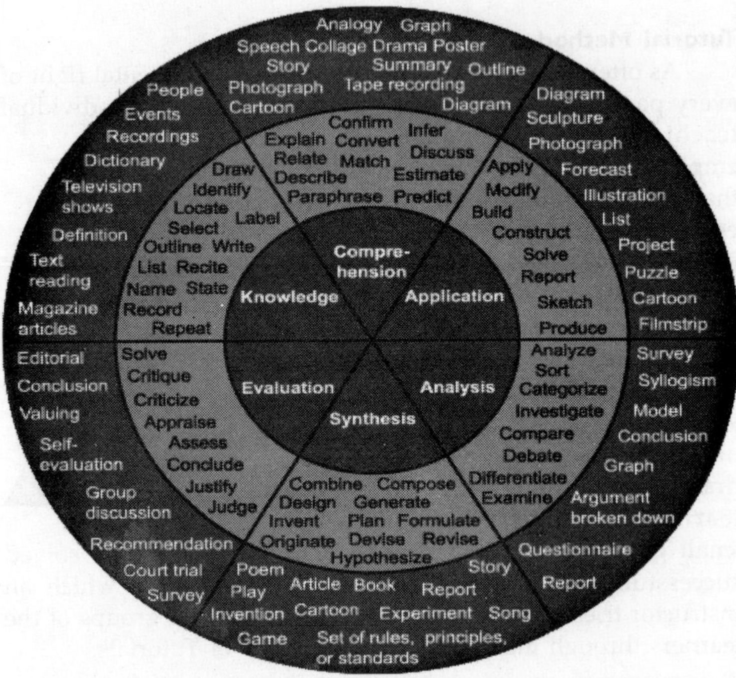

If a tutorial acquires the form of a lecture, then it will be considered as autocratic strategy. Contrary to this, if the learners are more active than the instructor, it will occupy its place in democratic strategies. Prof. Bloom's view is that the discussion should be based on the problem and the instructor should help the learner to the maximum to solve the problem.

Discussion Method

In the discussion method, the instructor motivates the learners to think over some problems by the way of questioning. After gaining motivation, the learners answer certain questions of the instructor or respond in some or the other way. The instructor develops his lesson by discussions, answers and some responses of the learners. As the need arises, the instructor helps the learners in solving the problem. Thus the discussion method is an active oral method in which opportunities of interaction arise between the learners and the instructor. As a result of this interaction, a change occurs in the attitude, feelings and motivation of the learners. Hence, psychologically and sociologically, discussion is an appreciable method for social learning and development of the learners.

Discussion is of Two Types

1. Formal discussion is adopted to gain pre-determined objectives. Hence, its principles are also pre-determined. It is essential to follow these principles in any condition.
2. Informal discussion is not pre-determined. There is no need to follow any principle to participate in informal discussion. The class-room discussion is an informal discussion.

HEURISTIC METHOD

What is Heurism?

The word heurism has been derived from the Greek word Heurisco which means I discover. Thus, heurism or heuristic method is that in which the learners search out the knowledge themselves by keeping themselves physically and mentally active. Learners learn themselves. The instructor

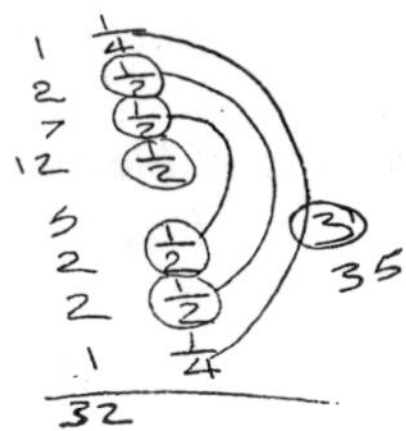

creates an environment where problem arises before the learner All the learners think about the problem, and in the end they conclude some result. Thus, all the learners find out truth by their own way. In this method the instructor creates problems before his learners, present suitable material in order to solve the problem and provides necessary guidance so that they may search out new knowledge by solving the problem as a result of making use of books, devices and other resources of his choice. Armstrong developed inductive method for science subjects by keeping in mind the basic principles of inductive method, but this method can also be used in teaching History, Geography, Mathematics and Grammar, etc.

Steps in Heuristic Method

1. *Creation of problem*: The instructor presents a problem to the learners in such a way so that every pupil may come to know about that.
2. *Discovery of facts:* The instructor presents various books, devices and other necessary equipments in order to solve the problem. He also guides them so that may collect the problem-related facts.
3. *Formation of hypothesis*: The pupil forms various hypothesis for solving their problems after collecting the facts.
4. *Testing of hypothesis*: The learners collects facts by experiments in favour of or against the hypothesis. They test the hypothesis by considering many false facts as the basis.
5. *Drawing conclusion*: The pupil accept only true hypothesis and leaves the false one. This conclusion is known as their discovered knowledge according to which the principles and laws are formulated.

Merits of Heurism or Heuristic Method

- Learners learn by doing themselves. Hence, it is a psychological method of teaching.
- In addition to the mental and' reasoning powers,

development of self-confidence and intellectual inter-dependence etc. also occurs gradually. This prepares learners to solve any problem likely to arise in future life.

- This method does not allow the learners for cramming of readymade knowledge.
- Learners work themselves and consult themselves. This coordinates their physical and mental powers.
- The entire task is completed in laboratory. This solves the problems of home work automatically.

Demerits of Heurism or Heuristic Method

It is useful only for the learners of higher classes and not for lower class learners. It cannot be used in nursery and primary classes. In higher classes too, it can be used only by the talented learners. The average or backward learners either get frustrated or they accept the decisions of talented learners while using this method. The modern culture and civilization has become so much complicated that every pupil cannot acquire knowledge by doing research himself.

The instructor has to provide its knowledge directly. The knowledge of all the subjects of a curriculum cannot be imparted to the learners for examinations by heuristic method. Hence, in view of present curriculum and examination system, this method is not appropriate.

It is evident from the above mentioned merits and demerits of heuristic method that it is more useful for the grown-up learners of rich countries. Its use provides the learners' opportunities of reasoning, thinking, observation, testing and decision-making by self-activity. These make them successful in acquiring the new knowledge.

ASSIGNMENT

Meaning of Assignment

The assignment means the task to be done by the learners at home. Through home assignments, the acquired knowledge is made permanent. The knowledge acquired in school is given to the learners to read, write and learn by heart.

Importance of Assignment

1. Assignments are used for infusing the need of motivation in the learners. In class, learners get hardly any opportunity to utilize the new knowledge. The home assignment provides maximum motivation to use the acquired knowledge and the assignments should be marked and returned back to the individual learner secretly without disclosing the grades to other learners.
2. Assignments help learners in developing a self-study habit. While doing the home assignment, the learners have to write the answers of the questions themselves. Hence, they bring books of various subjects at home from the library to study them. This study of the books develops the habit of self-study among the learners. The desirable attributes like self-confidence and self-reliance also develop among them.
3. *Encouragement of Self-Activity* : The learners get opportunities to express their views by self-activity. This develops their power of expression.
4. *Guidance in Learning* : Properly planned assignment helps in guidance. The learners and the instructor gain success in achieving educational objectives.

Types of Assignment

1. *Informative*: It is such a home assignment in which the learner collects various types of information, such as, the learners should be ordered to reply the following questions:
   (i) What are the main industries of Karnataka?
   (ii) At what places the sugar mills are located in Haryana?
   (iii) Who founded Calcutta?
2. *Problematic*: It is an assignment in which the learners search out the solution of some problems themselves.
3. *Memorization Type*: It is a home assignment in which the learners try to cram the already read lesson, e.g.,

the learners should be directed to learn any poem of the book by heart.

4. *Study Type*: In this, learners are asked to prepare a note on some topic.
5. *Average*: It is that assignment which any learner can attempt. In other words, average home work has to be done normally by each and every learner.
6. *Achievement Level Type*: This type of assignment is given to the learners according to the individual variations of the learners, in other words, more problematic and sufficient home assignment is given to the learners having sharp intelligence and simpler and limited home assignment is given to the mentally retarded learners.
7. *Practice Assignment*. In this assignment, learners are made aware of their previous knowledge. In such assignments, learners are given such questions to which they are to write answers at home.

CHARACTERISTICS OF GOOD ASSIGNMENT

1. A good assignment has one or the other purpose. Purposeless assignment fails to make the learners interested in doing that task.
2. A good assignment motivates the learners to acquire, new knowledge. Hence, the home assignment should be such that the learners, get motivated themselves for accomplishing. They should not take up it just to avoid punishment or to get some reward.
3. A good assignment creates curiosity among the learners. Under the influence of this curiosity, the learners become active and they accomplish the assignment.
4. A good assignment is definite and clear. At the very first sight, it becomes clear to the learners what they are to do and how much they are to do. Unless and until they do not get clear and have definite idea of the home task, they do not like to do it. Hence, it must be made easy and clear to the learners.

5. A good assignment is according to the interests, attitudes and the natural tendencies of the learners. Hence, the interests, capabilities and tendencies of the learners must be looked after while providing home assignments, otherwise they won't show full interest in completing that home assignment.
6. A good home task is related to the previous knowledge and experiences of the learners. If the home task is not related to the previous knowledge of the learners, they cannot acquire the new knowledge conveniently.
7. A good home task is based on individual differences. Hence, the intelligence quotient, interests and aptitudes of the learners should be considered while assigning the home task. If the home task will not be according to the mental level of the learners, they will not be able to finish it. The objective of the home task will not be achieved. From this point of view, sharp-minded learners should be assigned comparatively more complex and sufficient home task.
8. A good home task is accurate and proper with regard to the language, subject and validity. Hence, all these things should be cared while framing the home assignment.
9. A good home task is related to the learnt lesson. Home task makes the main points permanent. From this angle, the home assignment should be useful and appropriate in the practical life of the learners.
10. A good home task is challenging for a pupil. Hence, the achievement level of the pupil should be considered while assigning the home task so that they can utilize their mental ability to the maximum.
11. A good home task is related to the real problems of the learners' life. Hence, the home task must be related to the real life of the learners, otherwise they won't like to finish it.
12. The instructor issues instructions to do a good home task. He makes the learners familiar with the possible difficulties so that they may not lose the heart.
13. In a good home task, time factor is kept in mind. As the grown up learners can work for a longer time as

compared to the younger learners, the grown up learners should be assigned with the home work of longer duration while the younger learners should be assigned with the home work of shorter duration. From this viewpoint, the younger learners should be given interesting home tasks like shorter poems to learn by heart, to colour the pictures etc., so that they may complete it while playing. The learners, aged 11 to 13 years, should be provided with the home task which can be finished in one and half an hour. Similarly, home task should be given to the learners aged 13 to 16 years, which takes about 3 hours for its completion. The above planning can succeed only when different instructors of different subjects mutually decide the amount of home task to be assigned to the learners.

Brain-Based Learning and Emotions

By : Nellie Deutsch

Neuroscience has disclosed important information about the brain and how it learns. It has uncovered "unprecedented revolution of knowledge about the human brain, including how it processes, interprets and stores information" (Sousa, 1998). The new brain-based learning theory "require[s] that we now shift our focus to the learning process" (Sousa, 1998). This information can be used to "facilitate learning" (Jackson, 1999). This paper will discuss how technology can be used to support a brain-based finding that "emotions" are critical to learning.

How learners feel is very important to their learning process. When a learner is enthusiastic and doesn't feel stress, learning will take place. If the conditions are negative and the learner doesn't feel safe, learning will not take place. Neuroscientists discovered this information about the learning process as they were researching the way the brain learns.

Is the learning process the same as it was in the past? According to David Sousa, "yesterday's methods worked well for yesterday's students. But the student brain of today is quite different from the one of 15 years ago" (Sousa, 1998). It is therefore necessary to study how students' brains work today so that it is possible to enhance their learning. "Today's children spend much more time with television and other electronic media than with their parents" (Sousa, 1998). Technology can cater to these neuroscience brain-based findings in the computer lab as well as for online learning courses. Various Microsoft tools such as PowerPoint presentations, Excel, Word processor and other software with multimedia functions can be used by the teacher and students instead of using conventional outdated class tools. Since today's brain needs a TV like environment, both sound and animations can be used to suit today's learner. Lessons can be prepared by utilizing the information that is readily available on the internet. Learning can be meaningful. However to avoid frustrations and stress that can interfere with learning, lessons must be planned very carefully "to helps structure and focus students' explorations of the Net" (Deal, 1998).

This will direct them to the goals at hand. Today's students experience different "patterns" (DeJong, 1999) from those of the past. Brain-based learning findings reveal that "the search for meaning is innate..., occurs through "patterning"... and [that] emotions are critical to [these] patterning" (DeJong, 1999). Meaning must be based on previous interests and "emotions interact with reason to support or inhibit learning (Sousa, 1998). How students feel in the classroom "determines the amount of attention they devote to ...[the lesson] (Sousa, 1998). It is very important for learners to feel relaxed and safe in the learning environment. Feeling threatened will shut down the learning process and as Daniel Goleman claims, "hijack" the rest of the brain (Viader, 1996). Teachers can help students understand the impact negative and positive emotions have on learning. "Positive emotions such as love, excitement, enthusiasm and joy enhance the ability to process information and create permanent mental programs" (Sylwester, 1996). Learning cannot take place unless the learner feels "safe" (Sylwester,

1996). "Stress and constant fear, at any age, can circumvent the brain's normal circuits" (Viadero, 1996). And yet, emotions are critical to learning.

"Larry Cahill, James McGaugh, and their colleagues...have found that people were better at recalling stories or slides that had aroused strong feelings in them than those that were devoid of emotional context" (Viadero, 1996). Emotions can improve memory. Another finding was that emotions can either add or detract from learning. Since learning is based on individual patterning and experiences (Caine, 1997, p. 19), in this case electronic media, it is only natural that these environments be duplicated in school. Learning can no longer be limited to a single confined environment, such as the classroom. Teachers need to "establish an environment that is free from intimidation and rejection, high in acceptable challenge and where the learner experiences active participation and relaxed alertness" (Dwyer, 2002). This can be done by giving constant positive and encouraging feedback to the students while they are working in the computer room. Monitoring these rooms are much easier than in a conventional classroom. Each student has work assigned to him. Individualized lessons are possible so that each learner can find meaning in his particular assignment.

Computer-based learning such as project work (Deutsch, 2003) or working on Web Quests in teams of three or four is a great way to keep emotions alive. It is very challenging to work with others on a mutual goal. Since social skills are developed at this age, it is only natural for students to want to work in teams. This leads to many discussions and calls for decision-making. Students develop character and responsibility on the team. At the same time it is very important for the teacher to interact with the students to make sure that team spirit is high. If there are social problems some learners may feel threatened and uncomfortable. This will detract from their learning. Regular reflections and team discussions will help keep the team busy with their work. Daily journal reports are an excellent way to encourage both team and individual reflections on how students feel. These should be handed in regularly. Technology and computer work is very important. It's a challenge to do projects and learn collaboratively. However, feelings must be taken into account. Teachers must monitor the room at all times. Careful attention should be given to teams that are having difficulties. This gives the teacher a chance to sit with each team in order to discuss the team's progress and encourage the members to speak about how they feel. Feelings are part of the learning process. Students should learn about emotions and their importance to the learning process.

Teaching students how to feel enthusiastic about their assignments and projects will enhance their learning. Students can be empowered to find freedom in the Web instead of getting caught in it (Deal, 1998). It is up to educators to find ways of integrating brain-based learning with technology.

References

Deal, N. (1998, August). Getting teacher educators caught in the web. *T.H.E. Journal.* 26 (1), 50-54. Retrieved January 31, 2004, from http://proquest.umi.com/pqdlink?Ver=1&Exp=10-22-2005&VAULT=1&FMT=

DeJong, L. (1999). Learning through projects in early childhood teacher education. *Journal of Early Childhood Teacher Education,* 20 (3), 317-326. Retrieved February 4, 2004, from http://ecap.crc.uiuc.edu/info/pubs/katzsym/dejong.pdf

Deutsch, N. (2003). Nellies English projects: Collaborative writing projects. Retrieved February 10, 2004, fromhttp://www.nelliemuller.com/Collaborative_Projects.htm

Dwyer, M. B. (2002). Training strategies for the twenty-first century: Using recent research on learning to enhance training. Retrieved February 7, 2004, from http://www.tandf.co.uk/journals

Jackson, J. (1999, Spring). Issue theme: Brain-based learning. *The Reporter.* President's remarks. Retrieved February 2, 2004, from http://www.coe.uga.edu/gascd/newsletters/spring_1999.pdf

Rutter, T. Bringing the scientists to the educators: Mindful of students' brains: An interview with Eric Jensen. Retrieved February 10, 2004, from Brain connection: An online magazine. http://www.brainconnection.com/content/166_2

Sousa, D.A. (1998, December 16). Is the fuss about brain research justified? *Education Week,* 18 (16), 52, 35. Retrieved January 29, 2004, from http://www.edweek.org/ew/1998/16sousa.h18

Sylwester, R. (1996). Celebrating Neurons, ASCD. Retieved February 7, 2004 fromhttp://members.aol.com/Rss51540/brain2.htm

University of Phoenix (Ed). (2002). Learning and technology: Boston: Pearson Custom Publishir.g. Retrieved January 29, 2004, from https://mycampus.phoenix.edu

Viadero, D. (1996, September 18). Brain trust. *Education Week.* Retrieved January 29, 2004, from http://www.edweek.org/ew/1996/03brain.h16.

Gradation of Assignment

The home assignments should be graded at two levels—logical and psychological. The instructor should present the home task, first, in a logical sequence and then it should be graded keeping in mind the mental abilities, interests and developmental stages of the learners. Certain maxims of teaching must be used while the home assignments are graded. Those maxims are : (1) from known to unknown, (2) from concrete to abstract, (3) from simple to complex, etc.

DEMONSTRATION

Edgar Dale says that any conscientious instructor can, with a moderate amount of practice and a thorough understanding of principles, become skilful in demonstration. Good demonstration is good communication. Ordinarily the work demonstration means showing clearly by giving proof or example(s). Very often we demonstrate ideas, concepts, skills, attitudes, methods, etc. Instructors demonstrate how certain things are done, or how an engine works, and so on. They do this all the time without knowing that they are using the demonstration method. Teaching is all about communicating the right knowledge to the right learner at the right moment and this is based on the quality of offering satisfactory demonstration.

In Edgar Dale's Cone of Experience, demonstrations occupy the fourth place, i.e., after dramatized experiences and before the fieldtrips, followed by learner activities. Many instructors possess knowledge but they fail in demonstrating the knowledge in front of masses and due to lack in peoples skills, few instructors never succeed in leaving a long lasting mark on the learner community. We all know that offering right demonstrations would be seen as rare but rich learning experiences. Instructors very often resort to the demonstration method in the classrooms. The Chemistry instructor demonstrates how oxygen is prepared. The Physics instructor demonstrates how the white light gets refracted into seven colours, when it is allowed to pass through a glass prism. The Botany instructor demonstrates how sunlight is essential for the leaves to prepare chlorophyll. The Zoology instructor demonstrates with the help of a diagram or anatomical model, how the food is digested. The Mathematics instructor may demonstrate the use of logarithms in multiplication and division.

The Language instructor may point out the lip and tongue positions to demonstrate the production of a particular sound or sounds. The Geography instructor may use a globe and a candle light or torchlight and demonstrate how days and nights are caused due to the revolution of the earth on its axis. The History instructor may use chart or a blackboard diagram to demonstrate how a bill becomes a law in assembly or Parliament.

Characteristics of Demonstration

Indispensible

While teaching a skill, a demonstration through guided performance is virtually indispensable. No educator would think of any method other than this in teaching learners how to use the mathematical instruments, cultivate a garden, play a musical instrument, use SLR camera or perform experiments in the laboratory.

Need of Audio-Visual Aid

An effective demonstration requires audio-visual materials like the whiteboard, filmstrip, overhead projector, cassette recorders, charts, models, diagrams, etc. For example, traffic rules cannot be effectively demonstrated without using models. The Geography instructor cannot demonstrate without a globe, how days and nights are caused. If demonstrations are carried out without audio-visual materials, they become mere verbal explanations. Sound films and television are the most effective media for demonstrations.

Principles of Demonstration

Demonstrating a process, or the use of an apparatus etc., the instructor should create or we should say generate interest and arouse curiosity in the learners. Only when the instructor stimulates and maintains learner interest the demonstration will be successful. Learners want the instructors to be well prepared and it is expected that the instructor will perform the demonstration in a manner which would satisfy the mental needs of the learners.

Easy from the Observer's Point of View

1. The demonstrator knows his subject thoroughly, but the learners may only a very little or none about the subject, beforehand. So the instructor must plan and carry out the demonstrations in such a way that the concepts, ideas or processes etc., become easy and simple for the learners to understand and memorize.
2. There are key points in all learning, and the good instructor recognizes them. The experienced demonstrator puts special emphasis on them, repeats them, highlights them in some way. Recognition of the important concepts is very much expected from the instructor and transformation of knowledge is the key to the entire learning process of demonstration.

Stages of Demonstration

1. The Preparatory work.

2. The Performance itself.
3. The Evaluation.

The Preparatory Work

Demonstration is like a dramatic performance. The learners are to be kept interested and responsive. This requires the following:

1. Plan each Step (including Materials) extremely carefully. The instructor must make sure that every piece of necessary equipment is exactly where he wants it to be. A sudden interruption by the demonstrator (instructor) in the middle of the demonstration will spoil it. Think for example, a science instructor who stops the demonstration in the middle saying that he wants to go to the laboratory to bring the beaker which he has forgotten. A check-list of necessary equipment is a simple means of preventing such a situation.
2. Rehearsal, checking and rechecking is always a good thing, before putting up the show at all the levels. After organizing the procedure well, the instructor ought to test the demonstration for clarity, interest, duration and other elements with a good critic.
3. Outlines on the Whiteboard a must for grabbing attention of the learner . Though it is considered one of the very simple means of assuring that the demonstration will be understandable, should be planned in advance of the actual performance before the class. The whiteboard outline should be a logical sub-division of the demonstration into steps and key points.
4. Making Sure that Everyone can see and hear and this for the betterment of the instructor as well as learner. If the learners are unable to see or hear you during the demonstration, all the efforts put in by you would be of no use for the learner community. The demonstration will be successful only when the audience can see what the demonstrator shows and hear what he says. Proper lighting arrangement and

seating arrangement should be made. Theatrical presentation style would be best if the instructor is dealing with large classes.

5. Preparing Written Materials is necessary for giving learners something to ponder upon. Edgar Dale says, there is good evidence that learning through hearing and seeing is reinforced by written materials. Every learner in the class will find a review of the demonstration rewarding, for it is a kind of reconstructed experience or repeat-performance. The written materials should be given to the learners only after the demonstration is over.

Performance of Demonstration

Once the preparation for the demonstration is completed, the instructor is ready to start it. During the actual demonstration, he should do as given below:

"This has been really cool! If my dot.com company hadn't bottomed out, last month... I'd never have discovered the joys of substitute teaching!"

1. Communication is the key and this holds the way which could lead the instructor towards the chance of being liked by the learners. Information, knowledge and act of expressing the same knowledge is a must for any good instructor. As the instructor goes through the various stages of demonstrations he should keep learners interested and stimulate their curiosity.
2. The KISS formula is applicable also in teaching environment. Keep the Demonstration Simple. To keep the demonstration simple the instructor may include in the demonstration only important elements, omitting all the unnecessary details.
3. Do not Digress from the Main Points as this might not be taken positively by the learners who are not used to

your style of teaching. Digression from the main points of the demonstration spoils it. So during the demonstration, if a brighter learner would ask a complex question not related to the main points, the instructor should put-off the question for later discussion. If the instructor thinks it is really important for him/her to answer the question, the instructor may do so, keeping in mind the importance of time of other learners.

4. Check continually that demonstration is being understood by even the weakest learner in the class. While performing the demonstration, the instructor should watch the learners to know if they find any difficulty in understanding. If so, he may stop and clear up the difficulty and then proceed further.
5. Avoid dragging out the demonstration and try to spin the lesson all around the topic of attention during the class. The demonstration should never be so long as to make the learners tried. The lesson shouldn't be dragged out with unnecessary talking or aimless walking around the table. Exaggeration of any topic is not suggested and should always be avoided for remaining on the right track.
6. Keep Summarizing as this keeps the learners tuned in to your lecture. Using the charts, diagrams or the whiteboard the instructor can summarize. The key points should be clearly woven together so that they create a firm entity and the message is clearly transmitted to the receiver. As the instructor nears the end of the demonstration, he should restate the key points so that major idea emerge.
7. Provide written notes as these help the learners in revising whatever was taught in class. At the conclusion of the demonstration the learners are ready to look at the materials the instructor has prepared for their use may have written a step-by-step outline of what they have just witnessed, followed by the general conclusions and the key points.

INDIVIDUALIZED INSTRUCTION

In any conventional classroom there are more than forty-five or sixty learners and the instructor teaches all of them more less in the same way. Personally I have taught around two hundred learners in class and it had been very difficult to remember names of the majority of the learners, whereas the names of few who used to sit in the front row are always easy to recall for the instructor. Sometimes all the learners have to study the same content, in the same length of time, and have to take the same test or examinations. This kind of mass instruction does not take the following differences into consideration:

1. Needs and Interests of each learner are different and need to be understood by the instructors. Unfortunately in Indian context or we should say in Asian context it is hard for the instructor to give one on one attention to the learners. These also vary from learner to learner, so all of them will not have the same amount of motivation.
2. The learners also differ widely in their attitudes towards education. Some learners study out of liking for academic achievements, but many of them study out of compulsion. In our country the career of the child is decided by the parents and this is enough reason for the learner not to be motivated in the class.
3. The learners in any class differ widely in intelligence which determines the academic success to a very great extent. Broadly speaking there are three groups of learners, i.e., (i) those with average intelligence, (ii) those with above average intelligence, and (iii) those with below average intelligence. Mention should be made of different intermediate categories in each group. Level of intelligence though should not be mentioned or judged merely on the basis of marks obtained during the examinations, whereas the level of intelligence needs to be evaluated on the basis of life learning experiences of individual learner.
4. Special needs or we should say gifted learners is something which we don't normally talk about in our

country. With the expansion of ideas and views expressed in the media about the learners with special needs through movies like *'Taare Zameen Par'*. In our country many children of the school going age do not come to schools or even if they come, they drop out very early because the kind of group education imparted in our classroom does not meet their special needs or requirements. In our society learners with special needs haven't been given the right place and they still have to struggle for quality education. If these children are allowed to study what they feel useful to them and interesting to them, the number of admissions will go up and the number of dropouts will decrease considerably.

In the group instruction system, the speed is generally determined by taking the level of the average learners into consideration. The below average learners or the so called slow learners cannot cope with this speed and so they achieve far below their capacities. But the above average learners or the gifted learners do not feel any challenge and they also achieve far below their capacities. So what we need urgently is some kind of reorientation in our instructional system which will fulfil the demands of the individual learners because of the tremendous progress of Educational Technology. Some progress has been made in the West in individualizing instruction.

In their book, Fundamentals of Teaching with Audio-Visual Technology, Carlton W.H. Erickson and David A. Cur, have written that we talk a lot about individualizing instruction, but what can we really do about it? We can say an instructional system is individualized when:

(a) The characteristics of each learner plays a major role in the selection of objectives, sequence of study, choice of materials and procedures.
(b) The time spent by each learner in a given subjected area is determined by his performance rather than by the clock.
(c) The progress of each learner is measured by comparing his performance with his specific objectives, rather than with the performance of other learners.

Further, an instructional system is individualized to the extent that learners:

(a) Have, available in writing, the objectives, toward which they are working.
(b) Work toward a variety of objectives, at their own pace.
(c) Use a variety of materials and procedures.
(d) Move freely around the classroom.
(e) Talk freely to each other about their work.
(f) Pursue their objectives individually, with small groups of classmates, or with their instructors.

Also, an instructional system is individualized to the extent that instructors:

(a) Encourage learners to have a variety of objectives.
(b) Allow learners to move from place to place based on what it takes to achieve their objectives.
(c) Spend more time answering questions of individuals and small groups then lecturing to the entire class.
(d) Encourage learners to help determine the materials they work with and the procedures they follow.

Walter A. Wittich and Charles F. Schuller have given the following definition:

> Individualized Instruction consists of learning experiences specifically designed for individual learners on the basis of diagnostics procedures employed to determine individual interests and needs; once established, these learning experiences are largely self-directed, self-administered and within broad limits, self-scheduled according to the interests and convenience of the learner.

Elements to be Accommodated

1. How Learning Activities are directed or prescribed. Learning activities may be prescribed in considerable detail by the instructor or by the materials themselves or, the learner may have considerable latitude in

selecting his objectives as well as the methods and materials he will use to attain them.

2. A time schedule may set-up for an individual learner or for the subject matter he is studying; or he may have a large block of time schedule several activities within this time block, and use it without reference to a detailed schedule to study or work on whatever he wishes. Flexible scheduling and/or continuous programmes.

Individualization of Instruction bring a major breakthrough in educational system. One may expect educational technology to play a leading role in individualized instruction, with machines taking over those parts of the instructional and management processes which they can handle effectively thus freeing the talents and energies of instructors for the more creative and vital aspects of teaching learner development and the preparation of the software.

Role Playing

Role playing is the method in which four or five learners of the class or a small group of learners is allowed to imitate the experiences of others. The learners express their views in a natural manner through the various roles. Hence, role playing is a formal method in which learners are assigned roles without any practice and the learners play those roles happily in the class. Through the use of role playing method, recreating of the learners and expression of their emotions takes place. Their attitudes develop in a natural way by using this method successfully. In the teaching of subjects like civics, history, literature and science, etc. the cognitive objectives can be achieved.

Sensitivity Training

Sensitivity training method is that by which mutual relations of the learners are developed and they are made sensitive in respect of some problems. By awakening the sensitivity among the learners, their ego is awakened. They set motivated for solving the problem with their full energy. This method used for training the small groups of the learners. Such group meets once a week or thrice a month at the most. A programme is determined of participating all the learners of the groups in the debate. Instructor does not participate in the debate. He guides the learners as the need arises keeping in by the activities of the group.

Advantages

1. By appreciating the learners, they can be motivated for doing a task.
2. The social capabilities of the learners can be developed.
3. The tolerance and adjustment capability among the learners can be developed.
4. The behaviour efficiency of the learners can be enhanced.
5. A diagnostic understanding takes place as a result of interaction between the learners and a instructor.

REVIEW

'Review' means to think over certain main points regarding teaching:

1. Which lesson should be considered more important and which one is less.
2. To see how many lessons have been taught and how many lessons left.
3. To see errors in teaching and how those errors can be rectified.
4. What important points were included in the lesson and the points which were missed.
5. What points should be kept in mind so that the teaching objectives can be achieved.

After reviewing all the above points, an instructor succeeds in achieving the objectives of teaching and a sense to criticize develops in the learners. Hence, the instructor and the learner should both actively participate in reviewing. In review, the contents get consolidated in a systematized way in the brains of the learners.

What are the implications of the spread of English language education in China and Taiwan?

Yen-Mei Tsai

Date: 24/11/07

Module and code number: MMACOM_25 Education and Development in Asia

Module tutor: Kaori Okumoto

English has become a more and more important language in the world. This is because we need a universal language to communicate with other people when living in the global village. Moreover, the increasing significance of an English language is the consequences of the phenomenon of globalisation. According to Hwang (1965, 18), "English is not only for using in business, politics, and literature but also in science and academic research." Diwakar (2007, 2) also cites statistics indicating the use of English that "more than one billion people are believed to speak some form of English. … Three quarters of the world's mail is written and addressed in English and four-fifths of electronic information is stored in English. Half of all business deals are conducted in English. Two-thirds of all scientific papers are written in English." The great amount of people around the world including those people in mainland China and Taiwan has learnt English in order to communicate with others. We could understand the importance of English in mainland China and Taiwan from the standard of graduations being improved in these two countries. Nowadays, universities impose regulations that learners are required to take and pass an English language examination, for example IELTS (International English Language Testing System), TOFEL (Test of English as a Foreign Language), and TOEIC (Test of English for International Communication). Learners will only be qualified to graduate if they can get the expected score as required by their universities.

Unlike in other Asian countries (for example, Singapore, Hong-Kong, Malaysia and India), in mainland

China and Taiwan, English is not chosen to become an official language. The main reason is that, historically speaking, mainland China and Taiwan were not be colonised by any English-speaking country. Instead, a great number of populations speak Mandarin in these two countries. Diwakar (2007) states that although many people speak Mandarin, in comparison English is now used wider all over the world. Hwang (1965) assumes that if Mandarin is not too difficult to learn and if Chinese people could have taken the priority in science at first, probably Mandarin may have become the major language in the world at the moment, rather than English. Interestingly, people in mainland China and Taiwan are keen to learn English although their native language is Mandarin, which is a totally different language from English.

Except the reason of globalisation and English heat internationally why people are keen to learn English as mentioned before, why do people in mainland China and Taiwan do their best to learn English and regard their abilities in English as being so important? I will discuss this issue in my essay, based on materials mainly from books and websites. At the very beginning of this essay, I will define some terms which will help clarify the scope of my essay. Subsequently, I will discuss the implications of the phenomenon of the spread of English including the considerations of how English as a universal language spreads, and the factors which caused the spread of English. Also, I will do the comparisons between these two countries, and look at advantages and disadvantages of the spread of English language education through a "comparison" method. Moreover, I will use information as obtained from a radio programme for discussing the case of the spread of English and its implications in mainland China. I will also be based on my interviews with a Master learner in investigating the case of the spread of English and its implications in Taiwan. In the last part of this essay, I will provide some suggestions which, as I hope, will be useful for any further work on this topic area.

Definitions of "English" and "Education"

In order to make this essay as clear as possible, I would like to begin by defining these two terms, "English" and "education". There are kinds of English which are used in different countries, such as, in the United Kingdom, in the United States, in Australia, in Singapore, and so forth and of course they are slightly different in spelling systems, vocabulary items, and grammars; (John, 1997). "English", which I refer to in this essay includes all kinds of English as used in different countries.

In addition, both formal and informal types of education are all called "education" in this essay. Formal education includes all education from elementary schools to universities. Informal one includes cram schools and even the way people learn English by themselves.

As to the spread of English, I will look at the craze of learning English. Apart from English teaching in schools, people learn English in cram schools or by themselves. English learning has become a common activity nowadays. (Taipei City Educational Portal Site, 2008)

Why English is so Important?

According to Alastair (1995), there are over 60 countries in the world regulating English as their official or semi-official language and at a great number of important places people also use English in daily life. It seems that English is a tool used to communicate with other people who do not speak the same language, and obviously the spread of English is continuing. Nowadays, in a great number of countries people are keen to learn English because they realise the importance of English. They not only just regard English as a language which can be used in commerce, science, medical and technology, but also a language which could also be used for international communication. Moreover, it is crucial to use English to do trading with other people who can not speak the same language. English has become a universal language, and people know its functions and the necessity to learn it. After seeing the phenomenon of the spread of an English language all over the world, we could try to trace back to the implications behind that. Janina (2002) demonstrated Quirk's (1988) analysis that we could separate the varieties of the spread of English into three parts; that is, imperial, demographic and econocultural. Janina (2002, 10) continues to state that his imperial model, in which language is spread via the asserting of political control over colonized peoples...... At the same time, Quirk finds the basis of the spread of English to America and Australia in the migrations of English-speaking peoples from the British Isles. This basis has led Quirk (1988) to refer to this type of language spread under the 'demographic' model. Finally, he makes econocultural features of language, its combination of economic or commercial centrality and its cultural/intellectual role in the world community, the basis for his third model of language spread.

He pointed out a cause and effect. People commenced to speak English because of British colonisation. Then, there were more and more people who spoke English such as America, Australia and Canada. People have learnt economics since they needed to live in this world and they could do trading for example. Therefore, English has become important.

The Phenomenon in Mainland China

I will now discuss the spread of English language education in mainland China and Taiwan separately. To begin with, I would like to discuss the phenomenon (What is happening and why it happened? There is a saying, "Every why has a wherefore.") and give the happening example which is about the English spread situation, and the implication later on. Bob Adamson and Paul Morris (1997, 3) stated that in Comparative Education Review to express the change of English subject curriculum in Mainland China. "For Chinese Communist Party (CCP) leaders supporting Western-style 'modernization' policies (albeit with Chinese characteristics) the study of English is regarded as necessary for acquiring technological expertise and for fostering international trade." Facing the reality that learners should learn English as well as possible in order to take the superiority and to stand confidently in the world stage. There are five periods of curriculum change in Mainland China. The period one: the end of Soviet influence (1956-60), the period two: a search for quality in education (1960-66), the period three: the Cultural Revolution (1966-76), the period four: modernization under Deng Xiao ping (1977-93) and the period five: toward nine year's compulsory education (1993-) respectively, and the last period is the most important and impressive one. From the 1993 English syllabus in Mainland China, it mainly focuses on achieving economic goals and the main reason is that they think learning English plays an important role in developing economy. That is why they try to revolute their curriculum in order to enable as many learners as possible to learn more and more language, especially English. (Adamson and Morris, 1997)

Here, I would like to give an example as to how people including learners and ordinary people in mainland China are willing and ambitious to learn English. I will use information as obtained from the upcoming event Olympic 2008 in mainland China rather than interview a Chinese learner for example just like what I had done with a Taiwanese learner since Olympic is a big issue. For the upcoming event Olympic 2008, Beijing will be the place where the event takes place, consequently in mainland China it is the government's policy to speak English. (Lixian Jin and Martin Cortazzi, 2002) Owing to attempting to impress people from other countries and provide excellent services to foreigners who will participate in Olympic 2008 in Beijing, people in service industry including some shoppers and taxi drivers who need to serve customers directly have learnt how to speak English. They specially focus on the improvement of their abilities in listening and speaking English skills through taking some courses and listening to the teaching tapes even when they are working. In the following, I am picking up some parts from that conversation which was talked by hosts of English radio program (English Learning Craze in Beijing, 2007). Y represents to Yunfeng, and Z represents Zong Qiu.

Z_ As we are talking about the English learning craze in Beijing today, I have to mention one little anecdote that I encountered just a few days ago.

Z_ While I was shopping in the department store, I overheard several shop assistants discussing a question about English expressions. That was a department store where there are not many foreign customers now. They were talking about something like how to greet an overseas customer in English, by starting with "May I help you?" or "Can I help you?" People are really getting ready for the Olympic Games!

Y_ As far as I know, many people like these shop assistants are keen to learn English as the Olympics waits for no one.

Z_ English is a very handy language when it comes to communicating in an international event like the Olympics. It is no mysterious to me why there are so many Chinese people are showing a great interest in learning it.

Y_ I've talked to quite a number of taxi drivers who are also learning English, and many volunteers are also making their language preparations as well. All these are part of an ongoing English learning campaign that many Beijing citizens are participating to prepare for the 2008 Olympic Games.

Z_ We'll visit an ordinary Beijing residential community to find out what's going on with their learning experience.

Y_ All class members are with the community's English Association for the Olympics.

Z_ Most of the association members are retirees. The head of the community's English Association for the Olympics, Xia Fengzhi in his 60s is one of them.

Y_ Let's now listen to Xia Fengzhi about how he felt about these past six years and the Olympics. "Ever since we won the Olympic bid, more people joined in our community's English classes. In the year 2005, we founded the English Association for the Olympics. As the association expanded, I became more and more interested in learning English. Many of us are volunteers for the Beijing Olympics as well. So during the event, we will be helping overseas tourists with their shopping and sightseeing whenever needed."

Y_ His association has grown into the biggest of its kind in Beijing. The English learning campaign in Beijing is also encouraging more people to become more comfortable speaking English regardless of their age, occupation and education.

Z_ Hu Zhiyun is a new member and she wishes to do something for the first Olympics to be held here in Beijing, China. "By the time when the Beijing Olympics comes, I believe many foreign friends will come to visit Beijing. Not all of them can speak Chinese, I think, so it would be better for me to talk to them in a language that they can understand. English is a language that's widely used around the world, so I would learn to speak English so that I can tell them where to go if they want to find a certain place. At the same time, it will also be an opportunity for me to learn about their culture and customs, and enlarge my horizons about the world."

Z_ But I really would like to know who are teaching these Beijing residents English.

Y_ Let's meet one of them, Edward Ohlin, from the United States, who is now working in Beijing. He is a volunteer English tutor for the English Association in Tuanjiehu Community.

Edward Ohlin stated, "There is a passion now about learning to speak English. And I find the learners are eager and captive and interested in learning. People are interested in what's going on in other parts of the world."

According to this radio programme which was picked up by me, I could feel how English has become so important and popular in mainland China. People in mainland China learn English not only because it enables them to communicate with foreign customers and do their business, but also because it can help broaden their horizons to know more about other people's culture and custom. From this information, we could find out that the English craze exists not just in learners but in all citizen. Even a volunteer English tutor, Edward Ohlin, who is from the United States, can feel the passion of people in mainland China. Beijing Olympics really excites people's interests in learning English.

The Phenomenon in Taiwan

I will now turn to look at the present situation in Taiwan. Among the foreign languages taught in high schools, colleges and universities in Taiwan, English is the most popular one. (Ho, 2003) According to Chen (1996, 324), although English plays multiple functions in Taiwan, the stated objective of English language teaching in Taiwan's education system is confined to learning English for further studies, particularly studying abroad. Chen (1996, 324) also stated more recently that the reason for learning English was to help learners in high school and universities have access to the scientific and technological advances in the West. This is one of the benefits of learning English, which is an economic reason.

Sung, shih-hao (2004) divides his explanation of education into two parts: formal and informal education. In formal education, which refers in particular to school education, it has specific educational purposes and contents. As mentioned in the last paragraph, learners should learn English as a compulsory subject in the third year in an elementary school. Informal education is another type of education which people receive after the school education. For example, people can receive an information education through cram schools. There are a lot of cram schools in Taiwan which provide English lessons, these schools are known as "busiban" in Taiwanese. It is very common for learners to go to cram schools after the dismissal of a class. According to the statistics (see the table below) as provided by Kaohsiung City Government and as officially approved by Ministry of Education, the number of foreign language cram schools is increasing year by year. (Kaohsiung City Government, 2008) The reason why learners follow the national curriculum to learn English at their earlier ages than before is that English learning heat is more popular. Moreover, if anyone expects to have a better job, he/she is required to improve his/her ability in English language skills.

People learn English because not only they want to be more competitive for their career but also for being competitive and improving their ability to connect to the globalised world. Based on the electronic paper (2007) of the 241th volume as published by Ministry of Education in Taiwan, the authorities of the state enterprise believe that the authorities of the state enterprise choose people's ability in the use of English language skills to be the main criteria in deciding whether they want to employ the expectant or not. If you can speak fluent English, you can be more competitive in the society. People are encouraged to learn English in Taiwan. Why should we learn English, even though we live in Taiwan? This is a common and popular question which has brought up a great discussion amongst people. As to this question, some people might say learning English means you worship foreign things and fawn on foreign powers. According to the electronic paper, people who worship foreign things and fawn on foreign powers could not really speak English. In addition, some people refuse to accept this kind of people's behaviour; therefore, they raise this issue. From the electronic paper, we could learn that we could change from learning English to Chinese and we should promote it to let Chinese become a united language: Indeed, it is very crucial to have a language in common for people, but we do not live in the economic self-contained times anymore. On the contrary, we are facing economy which we have great dependency on and competition with other countries all over the world. We have no choice but help supply each other's needs if we would like to survive. Although the population whose native language is Chinese is highest in the world, English is the most widely used language. When people who do not speak the same language want to do international trade, they would use English to communicate with each other. Also, when professors write an essay, they prefer to choose English because their essay could be read by others easily. If they do not do it this way, their essay will not be as famous as may have expected. (Wu, yao-chou, 2003)

The statistic: The growing number of foreign language cram schools in the last ten years in Taiwan

(全國外語類補習班最近十年成長統計圖表)

Year: 2008	(number: 5363)
Year: 2007	(number: 5355)
Year: 2006	(number: 4979)
Year: 2005	(number: 4457)
Year: 2004	(number: 3896)
Year: 2003	(number: 3304)
Year: 2002	(number: 2778)
Year: 2001	(number: 2249)
Year: 2000	(number: 1784)
Year: 1999	(number: 1347

http://ap4.kh.edu.tw/afterschool/html/statistics.html (updated 15th January, 2008)

As a Taiwanese, I experience the craze of English learning in Taiwan. Therefore, I chose qualified method to demonstrate the English heat. In order to know more about what people think about it, I interviewed a MA learner, Miss Chen on 15th December, 2007, in my department of my university in Taiwan. She was sent to a private institution to learn the basic English language when she was an elementary school learner and the main reason is that there are a lot of people who overestimate their ability in communicating in English. Later on, English became a compulsory subject when she entered a junior high school. Some classmates of her even went to cram schools after the class for the sake of improving their English as much as possible, and this situation is getting more and more popular in Taiwan. Since all learners are normally required to pass the entrance examination in order to enter high schools and universities. Miss Chen is also required to do so.

Moreover, English has played a very important role when she took the examination, and in some cases the results of the English examination could determine which school she could enter and how good this school was. Furthermore, she noticed that government changed their policy that it was compulsory to teach English from the third year in elementary schools to senior high school. In her opinion, the government did that because they began to realise the importance of English. A lot of parents became aware of the importance of English; therefore, they sent their children to cram schools at the earlier ages of their children. Some of them believed that if children could start to learn English when they were little children, and they could have a good foundation of English. She thought that government changed their policy as a result of and which reflected the growing trend for the popularity of English. Moreover, I asked what she thought about learning English in our society. She stated that it was necessary and it was really important to have English ability. She needed it when she went travel, got the latest news, communicated with people who did not speak the same language, did international trade and so forth. In other words, it is better for us to learn English and to have a good English ability in order to live conveniently. On many occasions we should use English to make contacts with people. We could even receive the latest news and information which are written in English right away without waiting for the translation.

Compare the implications of the spread of English language education in these two countries—advantages and disadvantages

By comparing English education in mainland China and Taiwan, we can see that there are both advantages and disadvantage of learning English. I would like to discuss about advantages first. Because we need to use English to communicate with other people who do not speak the same language, that is why we should learn English in this case. For example, when we meet foreigners, we can have a conversation with each other. Also, when we go traveling, it is very crucial to speak English in order to obtain useful information. In particular, from an economic perspective, when we do international trade, we need to introduce our idea and programme to our foreigner partners. That is one reason why we need to possess an ability to communicate in English, in turn, this enables us to get a better job. In addition, most essays are written in English because English is the most widely used language in this century. If we would like to obtain more updated information, we should possess an ability to communicate in English in order to understand it. Therefore, we could always know what happen in the first place. It is an interesting phenomenon that people in mainland China have been trained to speak English in order to prepare themselves for the upcoming of Olympic 2008. This event will be held in Beijing. Why are people so keen to learn English? They realise that if they wish to build up their business and gain benefits, they should have the ability to communicate with foreign customers to know what they need because it is virtually impossible that all the foreigners might be able to speak Mandarin. We could see that English is a language for people to communicate.

Apart the above advantages, there are some disadvantages that I will turn to discuss now. Some people might wonder why people in the world have learnt English rather than Mandarin although Mandarin speaking population is more than English-speaking population. Probably, the main reason of the significance of English is the British colonisation of other countries. As I showed what Quirk's model previously, he demonstrated that English-speaking population had increased because of British colonisation. The United Kingdom was the most powerful country which colonised a lot of countries; consequently, the countries which were colonised by the United Kingdom took English as official language. Therefore, people realise that speaking English can help them feel convenient wherever they go. However, I do not wish to expand on this issue in this essay.

What is more, in these two countries, children are asked to learn English to prove they are elite. We could see from the entrance examination. If learners could get high score in English subject, they will have more opportunities to enter a good school. Therefore, some people started to worship foreign things and fawn on foreign powers. Also, in my opinion, some people place the high value of foreign culture and abandon Chinese culture. They are considered losing national identity. For some little children, they started to learn English when they were still very young. It is a dilemma. In deciding to study English, some of them may find it difficult to have a good foundation of Mandarin, so English can make them feel confused. There can be a lot of confusion between English and Mandarin caused by the differences between these two languages, for example their grammars and spellings are different from each other.

Conclusion

The questions of whether or not, and why, we should learn English are the big issues to people in mainland China and Taiwan. I have argued the implications of English heat in the world and pointed out how important English is in this essay. Besides, I have discussed the craze in mainland China and Taiwan and have done the comparisons of English education between these two countries. Therefore, I found out that the situation in these two countries is quite similar. Whatever the reason people in these two countries are learning English, the fact is that they are learning English for having a better life. Most of the people are keen to learn English with their own reasons. They understand that learning English has been a popular trend all over the world, and if they want to compete with other people, they should at least possess this ability. According to Alastair (1995), there are over 60 countries in the world regulating English as their official or semi-official language. People in a number of important places also use English in their daily life. It seems that English is the tool used to communicate with other people who do not speak the same language and obviously the spread is continuing. Nowadays, people in a great number of countries are keen to learn English because they realise the importance of English. They not only regard English as a language which can be used in commerce, science, medical and technology, but also a language which could also be used for international communications and a crucial way to do trade with other people who do not speak the same language. English has become a universal language, and people know the function and the necessity to learn it. We should try to trace back to the factors behind that after seeing the phenomenon of the spread of English language all over the world. According to Quirk's (1988) analysis, which was separated into three parts—imperial, demographic and econocultural, these are the first steps why English-speaking population is higher and English has been introduced to a lot of countries widely. Although mainland China and Taiwan have never been colonised by British people, they have still been influenced by English heat.

It is necessary to learn English and we could use it in practice. English has become a a tool used by people for communicating with others. It is also interesting to know other cultures and customs through English. We learn English because it is useful and it is worth learning. A proverb says, "Every why has a wherefore." There are a lot of advantages for us to learn English after analysing it. Living in a global village, we can not live only with a limited view of this world. On one hand, we understand that learning English is better than not to learn, so we should keep going. On the other hand, we should know the purpose of learning English. Language is a tool for communicating but not a tool for abandoning our own culture and look down on people who do not speak English. Last but not least, this topic is always an interesting topic for people to think about. If I have an opportunity to do any further research on this issue in the future, I would try to extend it by investigating whether or not people who possess an ability to communicate in English are more likely to have a better job and live happily.

References

Alastair, P. (1995). English in the world/The world in English in James, W. Tollefson. (ed.) Power and inequality in language education, Cambridge Press.

Chen, Su-chiao. (1996). The spread of English in Taiwan. Proceedings of the 13th Republic of China TEFL, Tsing Hua, October 1996.

Diwakar Sharma (2007). Teaching English as a second language, Deep and deep. p. 2.

Donald J. Ford (1998). The twain shall meet: The current study of English in China, British Library.

Electronic paper (2007). Volume: 241, online at http://epaper.edu.tw/e9617_epaper/foreword.aspx?period_num=241 (updated 15th December 2007).

English Learning Craze in Beijing, online at http://english.cri.cn/4026/2007/08/25/167@266128.htm (updated 14th November 2007).

Ho Wah Kam (2003). English language teaching in east Asia today: An overview. Times Academic Press (2003). English language teaching in east Asia today: changing policies and practices in Ho Wah Kam and Ruth, Y.L. Wong (ed.), Singapore: Eastern Universities Press.

Janina Brutt-Griffler (2002). World English: a study of its development, Multilingual Matters. pp. 9-10.

John H. (1997). Language is power: the story of standard English and its enemies, Faber and Faber, London.

Lixian, J. and Martin, C. (2002). English language teaching in China: A bridge to the future, Routledge.

Mei-shu, H. (1965). The teaching of English in Taiwan as viewed from the point of view of the use of English in the society: suggestion for improvement in the light of study of modern language teaching, unpublished MA dissertation, University of London, Institute of Education. pp. 17-19.

Quirk, R. (1988). The question of standards in the international use of English in P.H. Lowenberg (ed.) Language spread and language policy: Issues, implication, and case studies (GURT, 1987), pp. 229-241, Washington, DC: Georgetown University Press.

Sung, shih-hao (2004). Education survey, Wu-nan. Taipei City Educational Portal Site, online at http://www.tp.edu.tw/feature/200503_english.jsp (updated 12th January, 2008).

Bob, A. and Paul, M., The English Curriculum in the People's Republic of China. *Comparative Education Review*, Volume 41, n. 1, pp. 3-26, Feb. 1997.

Wu, yao-chou (2003). Why should we learn English well?, National Taiwan University.

Teaching/Learning Strategies

TEACHING STYLE INVENTORY

For each of the following situations, circle the alternative action which most closely resembles the one you would make. As an instructor you are required to select a specific course in regard to your responses.

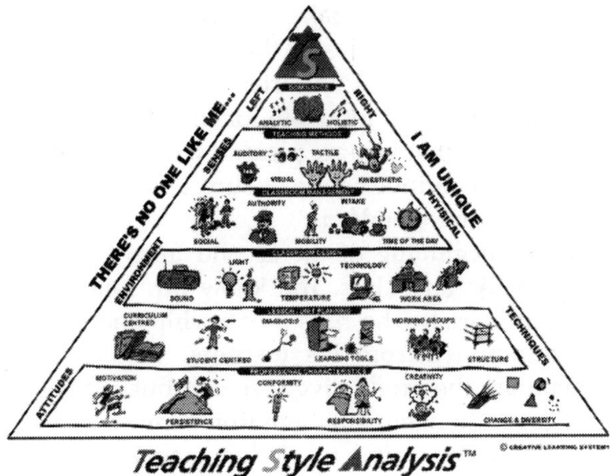

Teaching Style Analysis™

1. The semester is almost over, your learner's work is in a tailspin as their workload increases and final exams approach.
   (a) Emphasize the use of good study skills and time management techniques.
   (b) Let your learners know you are available for discussion but don't push.
   (c) Consider this as part of the learning process and do not intervene.
   (d) Take class time to help learners set goals.
2. A small group of learners working together on a major project are unable to solve a problem themselves. Group performance and interpersonal relations have been good.
   (a) Involve the group and together engage in problem-solving.
   (b) Give minimal direction and let the group work it out for themselves.
   (c) Encourage the group to work on the problem, reassure them of their abilities to find a solution and make yourself available for discussion.
   (d) Act quickly and firmly in an unbiased manner.
3. You have placed high standards on the quality of your learner's weekly assignments. Their performance is steadily improving week to week.
   (a) Encourage but take no definite action.
   (b) Strongly emphasize their accomplishments, make the group feel important and involved.
   (c) Continue to motivate for maximum performance.
   (d) Show that you are pleased with the improvements but continue to make sure all learners are aware of your standards.
4. At the beginning of the second term you inherit Mr. Robert Acton's class. You know Mr. Acton to be strict disciplinarian who runs a tight ship and gets excellent productivity from his learners. You would like to maintain the productive situation but at the same time begin to humanize the environment.
   (a) Take class time to conduct team building exercises

(b) Maintain rules of discipline and emphasize group tasks.
(c) Carry on as usual but model desired behaviour by being friendly and open.
(d) Let well enough alone; group building will occur naturally.

5. Several learners have requested that they be allowed to do a major term project rather than attend classes and take the course in the usual way. These learners have generally demonstrated good work habits.
   (a) Allow the change but provide strict guidelines and monitor closely.
   (b) Acquire the class's approval and allow the group to implement change.
   (c) This is exactly the kind of initiative you want your learners to display; agree readily.
   (d) Draft a set of guidelines for the project and offer this alternative to any interested learners.
6. Homework assignments are not being completed by your class. Learners seem unconcerned about meeting assignment deadlines. Re-scheduling deadlines has helped in the past but they continually need reminding to get work in on time.
   (a) Articulate the problem for the class and ask them to come up with a solution.
   (b) Incorporate recommendations from the class but then take charge and ensure rules are being followed.
   (c) Be sure your learners are aware of consequences, then leave it up to them to adjust.
   (d) Decide on the rules of the game: give the class direct, precise guidelines and then supervise closely.
7. Class performance and interpersonal relations are good. You feel however that the learners often get off track and during class discussion; you feel uneasy about your lack of control in these situations.
   (a) Discuss the situation with the class then introduce ground rules for class discussions.

(b) Leave the class alone, let them discuss issues they feel are relevant.
(c) Take firm steps to direct class discussions in a well-defined manner.
(d) Be careful of hurting learner-instructor relationship by being too directive.

8. You announce an unavoidable change to the best schedule half-way through the semester. The class is most upset and argue that the new schedule is unfair since it allows for less study time between exams.
(a) Permit the group to redefine its own schedule within strict parameters.
(b) Be sympathetic but stick to the new schedule.
(c) Turn the problem over to the class, let them give you the solution.
(d) Listen to the group's input, then you redefine the exam schedule before the next meeting.

9. Not much work is getting done in your class. Attendance is poor and sessions have turned into a social gathering. You feel that this group has potential to do well if they would apply themselves.
(a) Define the problem for demand they work it out for themselves.
(b) Ask for input from the class then implement strategies for correcting the situation.

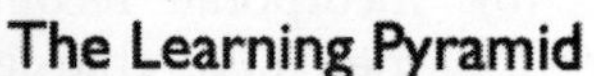

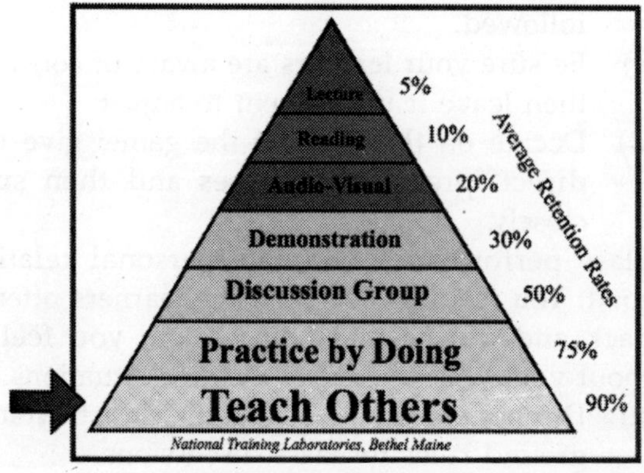

(c) Lay down the law-things have gone far enough and need a strict hand.

(d) Point out the obvious results of the class's behaviour then leave it up to the class to make to make changes.

10. The results on the latest test were extremely poor. The class is generally non-responsive and provides little feedback as to their difficulties.
    (a) Schedule extra review classes.
    (b) Ask the class to help define the problem and to generate solutions.
    (c) Discuss the poor results with the class then make it clear what is to be done.
    (d) Suggest what changes are needed to correct the problem, then leave the decision for change up to them.

TEACHING STYLE INVENTORY CHECK BOX

Circle the letter that you have chosen for each situation. Total each vertical line and note your predominant style.

	1	A	B	C	D
S	2	D	A	C	B
I	3	C	A	D	B
T	4	B	D	A	C
U	5	C	B	D	A
A	6	B	D	A	C
T	7	A	C	B	D
I	8	C	B	D	A
O	9	C	B	D	A
N	10	B	D	A	C
S	STYLE	1	2	3	4
	TOTAL				

Style 1

The role of the instructor as *Director* is to provide structure to the class. Emphasize step-by-step procedures for solving problems and provide precise directions regarding the work to be done. This instructor would probably stress attendance, homework, and be task oriented. He or she would probably be very well organized and well prepared for class. The teaching methods used most commonly would be the lecture and demonstration.

Style 2

The role of the instructor as *Coach* is to provide some structure to the class while at the same time, providing support and encouragement for the learners. This instructor would make an effort to establish close relationships with learners by encouraging out of class meetings and by being available for extra help or counseling. Firm but fair would be this instructor's motto. Typical classroom activities would include providing supportive feedback to learner through frequent evaluation, questioning, and one-on-one seat work.

Style 3

The role of the instructor as *Facilitator* is to involve the learner in every phase of teaching/learning process. He or she would often act as an equal participant, contributing to the discussion and encouraging others to contribute also. The emphasis is on creating a climate that is non-threatening; a climate in which learners feel at ease and free to experiment with new ideas. Typical classroom activities include: group discussions, role-playing, self and peer evaluations, and group projects.

Style 4

The role of the instructor as a *Resource* is to provide learners with the appropriate resource material so that they can take the responsibility for their own learning. This instructor would give recognition for noteworthy accomplishments and act as a liaison with other college support areas such as counseling and learning resource centres. Typical class activities would include: assigned readings, individualized projects, learner research assignments and learner presentations.

TRUE COLOURS AND TEACHING/ LEARNING STYLES

The true colours philosophy recognizes the four innate systems which drive behaviour and through which individuals strive to experience self-esteem. The True Colors model was developed in 1979 by Don Lowry which explores Dr. David Keirsey's temperament theory, based upon the research for the Myers-Briggs type indicator.

Don was an instructor who felt that temperament theory would be useful and interesting to his learners but he felt that it needed to be presented in a colorful and entertaining way to have the greatest impact on people. His vision was to integrate entertainment and education in what he called "edutainment" model. Don hoped to reach everyone through the system which focused on the uniqueness of each person as well as on positive qualities and strength.

Don's first love is live theatre and he uses colors to represent the four temperament types because colours are visual and were easy to remember. The colours were chosen for their association with psychological needs. Colors were chosen which had no cultural or negative connotation. True Colors is being used today with great success and enthusiasm by counselors, administrators and instructors, to name but a few. The model is powerful multi-dimensional tool which is innovative vehicle for change.

TEMPERAMENT TYPES

BLUE	GREEN	GOLD	ORANGE
The color Blue represents calm, completeness and a sense of belonging. Blue is balanced, harmonious, and tension free. It gives a feeling which is settled and secure.	The color Green represents abundance, living, growing and developing. People who choose green as their primary color are in esteem way competent. They	The color Gold represents security, stability, and loyalty. People who choose Gold as their primary color are in esteem when they feel responsible and are of service to others. They	The color Orange represents energetic life, activity and vitality. People who choose Orange as their primary color are in esteem when they are

People who select blue as their primary color are in esteem when they are authentic. For them life is a dream in which they must find meaning. They are sensitive human beings, enjoy close relationships and possess a spiritual side to their nature.	are always striving for perfection and seeking to develop their full potential. They are complex individuals who possess great analytical ability. Although they do not express emotions openly, they do experience deep feelings.	believe in order and take pride in the tradition of home and family. They consider themselves to be the backbone of society and feel they must earn their place in their society by fulfilling responsibilities and by caring for others.	free to act on a moment's notice. They choose to be impulsive and prefer a hands-on approach to problem solving. They are often extremely skillful in a crisis and do things for the joy of doing.

GOLD COLOR

Personality Descriptors	*Skills*	*Values*
• Loyal	• Following directions	• Security
• Dependable	• Handling details	• Orderliness
• Prepared	• Coordinating	• Stability
• Sensible	• Doing routine work	• Reliability
• Punctual	• Planning	• Obedience
• Organized	• Producing results	• Accuracy
• Caring	• Managing Time	• Fairness
• Co-operative		• Doing things for others
• Responsible		
• Practical		• Home/family

ORANGE COLOR

Personality Descriptors	*Skills*	*Values*
• Doer	• Producing results	• Security
• Optimistic	• Repairing	• Home/family
• Eager	• Selling	• Doing things for others
• Friendly	• Persuading	
• Playful	• Responding to emergencies	• Fairness
• Active	• Using tools	• Accuracy
• Risk taker	• Improving	• Obedience
• Adventurous	• Trouble shooting	• Reliability
• Risk taker	• Creating	• Stability
• Flexible	• Physical coordination	• Orderliness

GREEN COLOR

Personality Descriptors	Skills	Values
• Analytical	• Problem-solving	• Objectivity
• Logical	• Designing	• Independence
• Curious	• Logical Thinking	• Orientation toward the future
• Inventive	• Reasoning	• Intelligence
• Insightful	• Researching	• Complexity
• Precise	• Planning	• Truth
• Independent	• Observing	
• Precise	• Achieving	
• Critical		
• Achieving		

BLUE COLOR

Personality Descriptors	Skills	Values
• Enthusiasm	• Listening	• Security
• Warm	• Counseling	• Orderliness
• Caring	• Teaching	• Reliability
• Flexible	• Creating	• Obedience
• Creative	• Leading	• Accuracy
• Appreciative	• Motivating	• Fairness
• Peaceful	• Performing	• Doing things for others
• Sympathetic	• Working as a team	• Home/Family

FOOD FOR SELF-ESTEEM

Teaching and learning both require intensive effort on part of instructor and learner. Teaching in itself is a field which needs the individual instructor to be knowledgeable and competent. Instructors are human beings and we need to understand the reality of life that mood swings and emotions do change, improve and harm the teaching style of an instructor. There are certain symptoms we can look for when we are having a bad day-chances are we might be running out of esteem. We can learn to recognize these characteristics, which are generally related to our particular color grouping.

Green	Blue	Orange	Gold
• Indecisiveness • Extreme aloofness and withdrawal • Snobbish, put-down remarks, and sarcasm • Refusal to comply or cooperate • Perfectionism due to severe performance anxiety • Highly critical altitudes toward yourself or others	• Lying to save face • Withdrawal • Fantasy, day dreaming, and tracing out • Crying and depression • Passive resistance • Yelling and screaming	• Rudeness and defiance • Breaking the rules intentionally • Running away and dropping out • Use of stimulants • Acting out boisterously • Lying and cheating • Physical aggressiveness	• Anxiety and worry • Depression and fatigue • Psychosomatic problems • Malicious judgments about yourself or others • Herd mentality exhibited in blind following of leaders • Authoritari-anism and phobic reactions

IDENTIFYING TRUE COLOURS

True colors uses color to identify four distinct perspectives and personalities and each color represents an individual's character. Most of us have a dominant color, influenced or shaded by the others. Please read the following conversation and indicate which of these characters you identify with the most.

Character # 1 "I have this new program for making this organization run like clockwork. Thirty-five years of research, together with a computerized network of state of art equipment will give us a head start on the new program. We can be first!—On the cutting edge".

Character # 2 "Sure, good material is necessary, but I just don't feel right about starting a whole new program Just Like That. I suggest that we explain the benefits of the program to the whole staff-first,—get their support!"

Character # 3 "As I see it, the world belongs to those who take action!—And action is my middle name. By the time the organizers have it organized, I'll have it done and ready to do something new! I say let's start it—NOW."

Character # 4 "I think a clear-cut, down to business mode will get us to the bottom line here. After all, this organization has been here a long time. It is our responsibility to see that promises are kept and that the program runs smoothly..."

I identify most with Character #__________ and the Character #______________. The character least like me is Character #__________.

Read carefully the following character descriptions. Which do you identify with?

Character #1 "I am an independent thinker. I look for explanations and answers. I value knowledge and understanding. I am generally cool, calm and collected. Intelligence, fairness and justice are very important to me. I am natural non-conformist. I live by my own standards. I am a problem solver. I use a systematic approach to resolve problems and achieve goals. I prefer to work independently. I enjoy new ideas and theories and I like to be recognized and appreciated for my competence in a subject. I enjoy discussion and try to influence others to make informed decisions. I love to be challenged."

Character #2 "I am warm and compassionate. I contribute a lot of enthusiasm and encouragement. It is important to me that I find meaning and significance in what I like. I tend to be dramatic and imaginative. I value warmth and harmony in relationships. I sometimes have difficulty with structure. I have a strong desire to influence and motivate others. Communication with support and caring is very important to me. I enjoy being part of the personal development of others. I value self-expression. I am devoted, energetic and sensitive. I seek approval. I "turn off" when conflicts arise and flourish in an atmosphere of cooperation. I am social and work best in a group setting."

Character #3 "I love fun variety and excitement. I act on a moment's notice. I am often described as witty, charming and impulsive. I value skill and courage. I am a natural performer, and I enjoy competition and exploring. I consider life as a game. I learn best by doing and experiencing (rather than by listening and reading). I love to *"take action now!"* I prefer a bold and innovative approach to solving problems. I spend little time in long-term planning. I welcome and seek change. I can work in depth on things that I consider to be important I prefer games and "hands-on" activities. I like to put things I have learned to immediate use. I have difficulty with routine and structure."

Character #4 "I have strong sense of what is right and wrong. I am often described as faithful, stable and organized. I am hard worker who is good at handling detail. I understand the need for rules and I respect authority. I value home, family and security. I learn best in and organized and structured atmosphere. I like to be useful and to belong and to be accepted. I take life seriously and prefer a practical approach to problem-solving. I like that the foundation of a subject must be firmly set before new ideas and theories are introduced I like things done in a timely and organized fashion. I want to be problems through before making decision or take action."

Character #1 is primarily motivated by INNOVATION (new ideas/technology).
Character #2 is primarily motivate by FEELINGS (compassion/adaptable).
Character #3 is primarily motivated by ACTION (impulsive/independent).
Character #4 is primarily motivated by RESPONSBILITY (Practical/traditional).

I identify with Character #____________ and then Character #__________. The character least like me is Character #__________.

Learner Learning Expectations

Teaching environment in India is still old and follows the old orthodox traditions. While dealing with faculty fraternity in India, I was able to sense protest from the faculty when asked to maintain a learner centered teaching environment. Many Indian as well as Asian instructors still like to maintain a difference between them and learners. Academicians in India like to follow the old school of thought and present themselves as authoritarians instead of friends with learners. Knowledge is one of most important tools available for sharing with the learner community from ancient times.

Learning Styies Comparisons to True Colours

Learning Styles	*Gold Structured*	*Green-Independent*	*Blue Interactive*	*Orange-Active*
(1)	*(2)*	*(3)*	*(4)*	*(5)*
Performance	Abstract	Global Abstract	Global Abstract	Concrete Sequential
Learning Systems	or Concrete	Global Concrete		
Learning Channels	Sequential			
Modalities	Visual Auditory	Kinesthetic	Visual	Kinesthetic
		Tactile	Kinesthetic	Tactile
		Auditory	Tactile	Visual
Kolb	Converger	Assimilator	Diverger	Accommodator
McCarthy (4-MAT-1980's)	Style 3 Common Sense Learner	Style 2 Analytical Learner	Style 1 Imaginative Learner	Style 4 Dynamic Perspective
Kiersey	Sensory Judgment	Intuitive Thinking	Intuitive Feeling	Sensory Perceptive

"APPARENTLY ALL MY CREATIVE JUICES HAVE SEEPED INTO THE LEFT SIDE OF MY BRAIN."

Asian faculty members want to be seen as the source of knowledge, who intends to be strict and like to show a stern and grumpy poker face to the learner community. Time is changing and we need to change our teaching style as per our learner learning expectations. Instructors need to learn and restudy the theories and different research work they have been going through and try to interpret new theories present themselves as a resource person always willing to share knowledge with the learners. Instructors need to present themselves as a mentor, as a friend and a role model for the learners and help them in fulfilling all dreams they have been dreaming to achieve since long time.

While comparing faculty members from India, China, South Korea, Canada, England and US it would be difficult to give an unbiased opinion on the overall personality and teaching style of instructors, my personal experience with Chinese instructors gives me confidence in Chinese education system. Chinese instructors are very hard working and provide lots of opportunities for the learners to enhance knowledge and develop their overall personality.

LEARNER LEARNING EXPECTATIONS

Orange

- Competitive Instruction
- Direct Application of knowledge
- Opportunities to Discover by Doing
- Physical, Fun activities/ Stimulation
- Variety of Instructional Strategies

Blue

- Open Interactive Atmosphere
- Opportunities for Self
- Group/Cooperative Learning Environment
- Opportunities for Self-Esteem/ Reassurances
- Recognition for being an Individual

- Recognition for Immediate Application
- Content-Applied Learning
- Imaginative/Creative Sharing Activities
- Open Communication Approach to Instruction
- Conceptual and Content Learning

Gold

- Structure with Clearly Defined Goals
- Traditional Instruction
- Opportunities to Share Responsibility
- Recognition for Being On Task
- Foundation of Subject Established First
- Routing, Rules, Directed Instruction
- Specific Content Learning

Green

- Theory Investigation
- Independent Instruction
- Recognition for Competence
- Conceptual Learning
- Opportunities to Explore New Knowledge
- Immediate Challenge
- Beyond Test Instruction

Learner learning expectations and Teaching Style Models do differ but the end result meets expectation of both the learner and the instructor. While teaching many times instructors ignore the basic fundamentals and when they try to show off knowledge to the learners they push the learners back and try to force self-professed supremacy on the learners.

TEACHING STYLE MODELS

Orange

- Unstructured Discipline
- Spontaneous
- Hands-on Immediacy
- Expects Learner Variety
- Learning linked "Here and Now"
- Variety of Action Experiences
- Emphasis on Relevancy

Blue

- Fair, Democratic, Discipline
- Nurturing Format
- Individualization, Cooperative Learning
- Expects Learners Initiated Learning
- Strong use of Variety of Materials
- Learning linked to Individual Needs
- Adjustable Lesson Plans per Learner Needs

Gold

- Firm Discipline
- Outlines Lectures
- Organized Routines
- Expects Learner Accountability
- Strong use of References/Text
- Learning Linked to Past Traditions
- Detailed Lesson Plans/Syllabus
- Emphasis on Traditional Content

Green

- Discipline Expected due to Interest
- Sharing of Instructor Research
- Lecture/Discussion
- Expects Critical Thinking
- Strong use of Outside Materials
- Logical but Changing Lesson Plans
- Emphasis on Futuristic Application

LEARNING MOTIVATIONS AND EMOTIONAL INTELLIGENCE

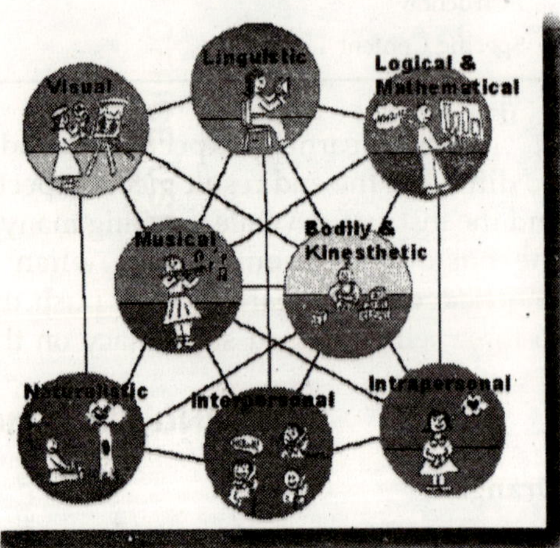

"Emotional intelligence" refers to the capacity for recognizing our own feelings and those of others, for motivating ourselves and for managing our own emotions and also of others along with managing our relationships. It is normally seen all over the world that people who are book smart but lack emotional intelligence end up working for people who have lower IQs than they but who excel in emotional intelligence skills. Successful entrepreneurs, business tycoons, managers and instructors do excel in emotional intelligence skills and they use these skills for developing relationships and expanding scope for recognition over all spheres of life. These two different kinds of intelligence-intellectual and emotional express the activity of different parts of the brain. The emotional centers are lower in the brain, in the more ancient sub-cortex;

emotional intelligence involves these emotional centers at work, in concert with intellectual centers.

Howard Gardner, a Harvard psychologist, in 1983 proposed a widely regarded model of "multiple intelligence." Gardner's list of seven kinds of intelligence included not just the familiar verbal and math abilities, but also two "personal" varieties: knowing one's inner world and social dexterity. Research and theories of the past indicate that a detailed comprehensive theory of emotional intelligence was proposed in 1990 by two psychologists, Peter Salovey, at Yale, and John Mayer, University of New Hampshire. Another pioneering model of emotional intelligence was proposed in the 1980s by Reuven Bar-On, an Israeli psychologist, in recent years several other theorists have proposed variations on the same idea.

Salovey and Mayer defined emotional intelligence in terms of being able to monitor and regulate one's own and other's feelings, and to use feelings to guide thought and action. While they have continued to fine-tune the theory, their model is being applied into variety of different models, Goleman has included five basic emotional and social competencies:

- *Social-awareness*: Knowing what we are feeling in the moment, and using those preferences to guide our decision-making; having a realistic assessment of our own abilities and a well-grounded sense of self-confidence.
- *Self-regulation*: Handling our emotions so that they facilitate rather than interfere with the task at hand; being conscientious and delaying gratification to pursue goals; recovering well from emotional distress.
- *Motivation*: Using our deepest preferences to move and guide us toward our goals, to help us take initiative and strive to improve, and to persevere in the face of setbacks and frustrations.
- *Empathy*: Sensing what people are feeling, being able to make their perspective, and cultivating rapport and attunement with a broad diversity of people.
- *Social skills*: Handling emotions in relationships well and accurately reading social situations and networks; interacting smoothly; using these skills to persuade

and lead, negotiate and settle disputes, for cooperation and teamwork.

Learning Motivations

Orange Learners

- Perform well in competition, especially when there is a lot of action;
- Love games and "hand-on" activities;
- Love fun and excitement;
- Have difficulty with routine or structured presentations;
- Perform best when they can apply skills learned in school to the world in which they live; and
- Learn by doing.

Atmosphere in which Orange Learners Learn Best

- Spontaneous
- Sense of humor
- Animated, active
- Lots of interaction
- Friendly
- Little lecture

Looking at Instructors for the Orange Perspective

Orange instructor: A good match with the Orange learner. The learner is likely to maintain the greatest rapport with a Orange instructor and the learner appreciated the atmosphere of freedom and spontaneity in this instructor's classroom and responds favorably to the "hands-on" approach to learning; both instructor and learner enjoy games and competition and are tireless in their efforts to complete any job at hand.

Gold instructor: The Gold instructor's demands for order, organization and appropriate behavior in the classroom do not conform well with the Orange learner's needs for spontaneity, fun, and quick action. The Gold instructor emphasizes rules and facts as well as neatness and structure. The Orange learner may react with various degrees of rebellion and hostility when confronted with Gold classroom atmosphere.

Green instructor: The Green instructor is often capable of creating an atmosphere of independence and freedom of thought and action in his classroom. This climate allows the Orange learners to express his needs and possibility to establish methods for learning in his own style. The Green instructor can also be perceived as too theoretical by the Orange learner. This can create the impression that the instructor is out of touch and unconcerned with the here and now.

Blue instructor: The Blue instructor can have some empathy for the Orange learner's needs, and this instructor's good sense of humor is protection from reacting too harshly to the Orange learner's demands for fun and entertainment. The Orange learner may require more "hands-on" activities, games, and competition then are normally scheduled in the lesson plans for the Blue instructor.

Gold Learners

- Do their best when the course content is structured and clearly defined;
- Want to know when they are on the right track;
- Are greatly helped by rules and directions; and
- Thrive on routine and orderliness.

Atmosphere in which Gold Learners Learn Best

- Structured
- Organized
- Tasks clearly stated
- Clear expectations

Looking at Instructors from the Gold Perspective

Orange instructor: This combination can be somewhat problematic, the Gold learner prefers organized, structured and predictable routines, while the Orange instructor ends to prefer an atmosphere of excitement. The Gold learner may often complain that tasks are never completed and that he does not learn much of anything in the Orange instructor's classroom.

The Gold learner strives for perfection and enjoys being validated for neat and accurate work.

Gold instructor: This is a suitable match, the Gold learner is likely to maintain the greatest rapport and cooperation with the Gold instructor. The learner appreciates the structure, organization, and rules that the Gold instructor emphasizes. The Gold learner responds well to this instructor's style of presenting material which is based on logical procedures and clearly defined factual information.

Green instructor: The Green instructor may not always meet the needs of the Gold learner for clear and concise rules and regulations. The independent thinking, originality, and mental creativity so valued by this Green instructor will not be highly appreciated by the Gold learner. The Gold learner may experience anxiety and difficulty related to grasping conceptual matter if it is not explained and demonstrated in concrete ways.

Blue instructor: The Gold learner responds well to the Blue instructor's classroom atmosphere if a regular and predictable schedule is maintained. The Gold learner requires rules and facts, as well as organized, accurate, and logical procedures. The Gold learner may differ from the Blue instructor in expression of or response to very deep emotions. Although the Gold learner follows rules and accomplished well structured work, the creativity valued by the Blue instructor may rarely be exhibited.

Blue Learners

- Feel best in an open, interactive atmosphere;
- Like to feel that their instructors really care about them and that they give the class a personal touch;
- Appreciate supportive attention and feedback;
- Thrive in a "humanistic," people-oriented environment; and
- "Turn-offs" when conflicts arise and flourish in an atmosphere of cooperation.

Atmosphere in which they learn best

- Warm

- Creative
- Personal
- Discussion
- Relaxed
- Flexible
- Freedom to experiment

Looking at Instructors from the Blue Perspective

Orange instructor: This combination can work well if the Orange instructor allows the Blue learner to be creative and show personal concern. The Blue learner appreciated the good sense of humor of the Orange instructor. The learner may have difficulty making quick decisions and could become bogged down before completing a task. Although the Blue learner values communication and social interaction, the Orange instructor's direct mode of criticism and comments may not be appreciated.

Gold instructor: The Blue learner adheres to the rule of the Gold instructor as long as they seem fair and there is personal consideration and compassion given to the learner. The Blue learner will cooperate, particularly if it is felt the Gold instructor likes and cares for the individuality of the learner. Unlike the Gold instructor, the Blue learner tends to be emotional and to allow feelings to interfere with academic work. This learner's need to socialize may also be viewed as highly disruptive by the Gold instructor.

Green instructor: The Blue learner responds well to the classroom atmosphere of the Green instructor, as long as it is personally relevant and stimulating to a creative imagination. The blue learner is motivated to perform in an effort to please the instructor, rather than to demonstrate intellectual mastery of a concept. Unlike the Green instructor, this learner tends to value feelings and interpersonal communication above ideas and concepts.

Blue instructor: The Blue learner will likely maintain the greatest rapport and consideration with the Blue instructor. The Blue learner appreciated the fairness, sensitivity, and personal concern expressed by the Blue instructor. The atmosphere of imaginative creativity and social interaction provided by the Blue instructor is highly appealing to the Blue learner.

Green Learners

- Perform best when exposed to the driving force or overall theory behind a subject;
- Prefer to work independently;
- Need to challenged; and
- Like to be recognized and appreciated for their competence in a subject.

Atmosphere in which Green learners learn best

- Academically demanding
- Energetic programs
- Encouragement to learn more

Looking at the Instructors from the Green Perspective

Orange instructor: The Green learner responds well to the classroom atmosphere of the Orange instructor if attracted to the subject matter and if allowed to express personal ideas. The Green learner is creative and enjoys discovering new ways of solving problems. Unlike the Orange instructor, the Green learner values ideas and concepts above immediate action and wants to inquire about the principles behind each task.

Gold instructor: The combination works only if the Green learner is sufficiently interested in the subject matter and given some freedom to explore ideas and concepts beyond the requirements of the class. Unlike the Gold instructor, the Green learner can be oblivious to rules and regulations. It will be difficult to gain the Green learner's cooperation without a perception that rules are logical and necessary.

Green Instructor

The Green learner will likely maintain the greatest rapport and cooperation with Green instructors. The learner appreciates the stimulating and creative environment provided by the Green instructor and enjoys discussing ideas, investigating relationships between principles, and discovering new ways of solving problems—especially in conjunction with the Green instructor.

Blue instructor: The Green learner responds well to classroom atmosphere of the Blue instructor, as long as the learner's interest in the subject matter and curiosity is continually reinforced. Unlike the Blue instructor, the Green learner is less concerned with the feelings of others and will tend to express opinions regardless of how they may affect the feelings of others.

Learning Environment

SETTING A CLIMATE FOR LEARNING

Climate in this context refers to the prevailing set of influences and conditions that characterize a group of learners in a learning environment. These influences and conditions can be classified into broad categories that might include learner behavior, learner prior learning, learner/instructor interaction,

instructor attitudes and behaviors, and environmental factors. Some influences are negative and detract from the living climate, while others are positive and result in a more meaningful, educational experience for all concerned.

LEARNING OUTCOMES

At the completion of this section, learners/participants will have:

- Identified activities that will invite learners to be involved in the learning process.
- Applied strategies to maximize learner's abilities to succeed.

LEARNING THEORIES—SOME STRENGTHS AND WEAKNESSES

What are the perceived strengths and weaknesses of using certain theoretical approaches to instructional design?

Behaviourism

Weakness—the learner may find themselves in a situation where the stimulus for the correct response does not occur, therefore the learner cannot respond.—A worker who has been conditioned to respond to a certain cue at work stops production when an anomaly occurs because they do not understand the system.

Strength—the learner is focused on a clear goal and can respond automatically to the cues of that goal.—W.W.II pilots were conditioned to react to silhouettes of enemy planes, a response which one would hope became automatic.

Cognitivism

Weakness—the learner learns a way to accomplish a task, but it may not be the best way, or suited to the learner or the situation. For example, logging onto the internet on one computer may not be the same as logging in on another computer.

Strength—the goal is to train learners to do a task the same way to enable consistency.—Logging onto and off of a workplace computer is the same for all employees; it may be important do an exact routine to avoid problems.

Constructivism

Weakness—in a situation where conformity is essential divergent thinking and action may cause problems. Imagine the fun Revenue Canada would have if every person decided to report their taxes in their own way—although, there probably are some very "constructive" approaches used within the system we have.

Strength—because the learner is able to interpret multiple realities, the learner is better able to deal with real life situations. If a learner can problem solve, they may better apply their existing knowledge to a novel situation. (Schuman, 1996)

Theory of Learner Involvement

How important is learner involvement to successful course completion? Who is responsible for learner motivation? Do faculty have a responsibility to reduce attrition rates, and at what cost to standards? Your answers to these questions will have an impact on how you conduct your classes from the very beginning. Alexander Astin offers some interesting insights into these questions. In his book, *Achieving Educational Excellence*, Astin presents a theory of learner involvement. Stated simply, he makes the claim that "Learners learn by becoming involved". For Astin, learner involvement refers to the amount of physical and psychological energy that the learner devotes to the academic experience. "A highly involved learner is one who, for example, devotes considerable energy to studying, spends a lot of time on campus, participates actively in learner's organizations and interacts frequently with faculty members and other learners. Conversely, an uninvolved learner may neglect studies, spend little time on campus, abstain from extracurricular activities, and have little contact with faculty members or other learners".

Astin considers two propositions in this theory to be the key educational postulates because they offer clues about how to design more effective educational programs for learners and few of the clues are as follows:

- The amount of learner learning and personal development associated with any educational program is directly proportional to the quality and quantity and quantity of learner involvement in that program.
- The effectiveness of any educational policy or practice is directly related to the capacity of that policy or practice to increase learner involvement.

"According to the theory of learner involvement, if a particular curriculum or a particular array of resources is to have its intended effects; it must elicit enough learner effort and investment of energy to bring about the desired learning and development. Simply exposing the learner to a particular set of courses may or may not work". In particular, Austin cautions about educational practices that tend to assign learners a passive role as recipients of information, and he emphasizes the active participation of learners in the learning process.

"In applying the theory of learner involvement, administrators and faculty members must recognize that virtually every institutional policy and practice can affect how learners spend their time and how much effort they devote to academic pursuits. Moreover, administrative decisions on many non-academic issues can significantly affect how learners spend their time and energy. Ultimately, these allocations of time and effort should have important effects on how well learners actually develop their talents".

CASE STUDY: THE OPEN UNIVERSITY VIRTUAL LEARNING ENVIRONMENT PROGRAMME

Tag: eGov Strategy Print article: Email article: This was published: 20 Mar. 2009—07:00 am *ShareThis*

This is a case study from a finalist in the *e-Government National Awards 2008.*

Awards category (10) e-Government excellence in Learning & Skills.

The Open University http://www.open.ac.uk

"Over the past three years the Open University has developed a new virtual learning environment for its many distance learners based on the open source system, Moodle. OU learners now have a robust system for managing their learning with interactive content and the ability to interact better using Web 2.0 technologies.

Meanwhile the initiative has had an impact far beyond the OU, with many colleges, universities and other organisations adopting Moodle partially as a result of the OU's decision to select it and invest Â£5m in a programme to enhance the software and roll it out across the institution."

"The OU virtual learning environment was delivered on time in three main releases during a development programme which ran from Oct. 2005 to July 2008. Extensive requirements gathering activities led to the development of major enhancements to Moodle, most of which have been fed back into the publicly-available version of the software now in use across the UK and internationally. Developments included enhancements to ensure that Moodle is accessible by learners with a wide range of disabilities. New functionality includes a new gradebook, an eportfolio system, a wiki optimised for use in education, and improvements for mobile learners such as a podcasting module.

The development of the software was accompanied by a major change management programme involving consultation, communications and staff development activities, resulting in a transfer of learning content and activities for the great majority of OU courses to the VLE.

By May 2008, there were 535 active courses on the OU VLE with more than 80,000 learners accessing the system. 14% of courses are now using interactive tools such as blogs and wikis. These figures are set to increase considerably in late 2008 with the release of new VLE-based level 1 courses in several popular subject areas.

Optimisations to the Moodle codebase and a robust supporting infrastructure have ensured that the system is available as planned more than 95.5% of the time.

The OUâ€™s decision to adopt the software is widely considered to be the tipping point for organisations who wished to move to an open source virtual learning environment.

Recent surveys have shown that 23% of higher education institutions and 59% of further education colleges in the UK are now using Moodle â€ "a dramatic change from three years ago when most institutions were using commercial VLEs."

The OU received a Mellon Award in 2006 for its â€œmassive institutional commitment to Moodleâ€ and recognised its â€œleadership in bringing Moodle to the next level of performance, scalability and enterprise-readinessâ€ â€ "see http://matc.mellon.org/winners/winner-2006".

Most development work on Moodle was carried out in-house however outsourcing also took place: â€¢ CatalystIT in New Zealand and pteppic.net in the UK provided initial support in using and developing the Moodle platform while skills were being developed in-house â€¢ Accessibility enhancements, improvements to the quiz module and a new roles and permissions architecture were outsourced to Moodle.com in Perth, Australia â€¢ Excelsoft India redeveloped the voting and podcasting modules.

Background: e-Government National Awards

The *e-Government National Awards 2008* recognise "best of the best" strategies, achievements, teams and individuals in UK public sector web, ICT & e-Government services. The Awards were presented 20th January 2009 in the City of London Guildhall by *Cabinet Office* Minister Tom Watson, MP, and Government CIO John Suffolk. Prime Minister the Rt. Hon. Gordon Brown, MP joined the awards dinner via video link. *Watch the Prime Minister's speech on YouTube at this link.*

The Awards winners are listed at this link.

Platinum sponsor was KPMG.

Also sponsors were O2, Directgov, and Jadu.

The Awards were supported by the *Government Chief Information Officer (Cabinet Office)*, the *Society of Information Technology Management (Socitm)*, and *SOLACE (Society of Local Authority Chief Executives and Senior Managers)*.

SENSORY STIMULATION THEORY

Traditional sensory stimulation theory has as its basic premise that effective learning occurs when the senses are stimulated (Laird, 1985). Laird quotes research that found the vast majority of knowledge held by adults (75%) is learned through seeing. Hearing is the next most effective (about 13%) and the other senses—touch, smell and taste account for 12% of what we know. By stimulating the senses, especially the visual sense, learning can be enhanced. However, this theory says that if multi-senses are stimulated, greater learning takes place. Stimulation through the senses is achieved through a greater variety of colours, volume levels, strong statements, facts presented visually, use of a variety of techniques and media.

REINFORCEMENT THEORY

This theory was developed by the behaviourist school of psychology, notably by B.F. Skinner earlier this century (Laird, 1985, Burns, 1995). Skinner believed that behaviour is a function of its consequences. The learner will repeat the desired behaviour if positive reinforcement (a pleasant consequence) follows the behaviour.

Positive reinforcement, or 'rewards' can include verbal reinforcement such as 'That's great' or 'You're certainly on the right track' through to more tangible rewards such as a certificate at the end of the course or promotion to a higher level in an organization.

Negative reinforcement also strengthens behaviour and refers to a situation when a negative condition is stopped or avoided as a consequence of the behaviour. Punishment, on the other hand, weakens behaviour because a negative condition is introduced or experienced as a consequence of the behaviour and teaches the individual not to repeat the behaviour which was negatively reinforced. A set of conditions is created which are designed to eliminate behaviour (Burns, 1995, p. 108). Laird considers this aspect of behaviourism has little or no relevance to education. However, Burns says that punishment is widely used in everyday life although it only works for a short time and often only when the punishing agency is present.

Burns notes that much Competency-based Training is based on this theory, and although it is useful in learning repetitive tasks like multiplication tables and those work skills that require a great deal of practice, higher order learning is not involved. There is criticism of this approach that it is rigid and mechanical.

COGNITIVE-GESTALT APPROACHES

The emphasis here is on the importance of experience, meaning, problem-solving and the development of insights (Burns, 1995, p. 112). Burns notes that this theory has developed the concept that individuals have different needs and concerns at different times, and that they have subjective interpretations in different contexts.

FACILITATION THEORY—(THE HUMANIST APPROACH)

Carl Rogers and others have developed the theory of facilitative learning. The basic premise of this theory is that learning will occur by the educator acting as a facilitator, that is by establishing an atmosphere in which learners feel comfortable to consider new ideas and are not threatened by external factors (Laird, 1985.)

Other characteristics of this theory include:

- a belief that human beings have a natural eagerness to learn,
- there is some resistance to, and unpleasant consequences of, giving up what is currently held to be true, and
- the most significant learning involves changing one's concept of oneself.

Facilitative instructors are:

- less protective of their constructs and beliefs than other instructors,
- more able to listen to learners, especially to their feelings,

- inclined to pay as much attention to their relationship with learners as to the content of the course, and
- apt to accept feedback, both positive and negative and to use it as constructive insight into themselves and their behaviour.

Learners:

- are encouraged to take responsibility for their own learning,
- provide much of the input for the learning which occurs through their insights and experiences, and
- are encouraged to consider that the most valuable evaluation is self-evaluation and that learning needs to focus on factors that contribute to solving significant problems or achieving significant results.

Experiential Learning

Kolb proposed a four-stage learning process with a model that is often referred to in describing experiential learning (McGill & Beaty, 1995). The process can begin at any of the stages and is continuous, i.e. there is no limit to the number of cycles you can make in a learning situation. This theory asserts that without reflection we would simply continue to repeat our mistakes. The experiential learning cycle:

Kolb's research found that people learn in four ways with the likelihood of developing one mode of learning more than another. As shown in the 'experiential learning cycle' model above, learning is:

- through concrete experience
- through observation and reflection
- through abstract conceptualization
- through active experimentation

DIFFERENCES IN LEARNING STYLES

As already discussed, the idea that people learn in different ways has been explored over the last few decades by educational researchers. Kolb, one of the most influential of these, found that individuals begin with their preferred style in the experiential learning cycle. Honey and Mumford (1986 cited in McGill & Beaty, 1995, p. 177) building on Kolb's work, identified four learning styles:

- Activist (enjoys the experience itself).
- Reflector (spends a great deal of time and effort reflecting).
- Theorist (good at making connections and abstracting ideas from experience).
- Pragmatist (enjoys the planning stage).

There are strengths and weaknesses in each of these styles. Honey and Mumford argue that learning is enhanced when we think about our learning style so that we can build on strengths and work towards minimizing weaknesses to improve the quality of learning.

CONSTRUCTIVIST LEARNING ENVIRONMENTS

In *Constructivist learning environments: Case studies in instructional design,* Wilson (1996) defines a constructivist learning environment as: "a place where learners may work together and support each other as they use a variety of tools and information resources in their guided pursuit of learning goals and problem-solving activities" (p. 5). He emphasizes learning environments as opposed to 'instructional' environments in order to promote "a more flexible idea of learning", one which emphasizes "meaningful, authentic activities that help the learner to construct understandings and develop skills relevant to problem-solving" (p. 3).

Riesbeck (1996) argues that "Constructivism is not a particular model of learning, however. It does not describe a process or set of mecanisms by which this construction occurs" (p. 49). Nonetheless, Honebein (1996) in his description of two learning environments, *Socrates* and *Lab Design Project*, illustrates how constructivist principles can provide a guide or framework to build constructivist learning environments. Drawing on the work of authors Cunningham, Duffy, & Knuth (1993), Honebein explains how *LDP* and *Socrates* were designed with pedagogical goals which provided the theory on which the design of the environments was based. These principles or goals can be summarized briefly as follows:

- Provide learners with experience with the knowledge construction process.
- Provide experience in and appreciation for multiple perspectives.
- Maintain the authentic context of the learning task.
- Allow for a learner-centred learning process whereby learners play an important role in setting the goals for learning.
- Provide for collaboration.
- Use multiple modes of representation.
- Encourage metacognitive and reflexive activities (p. 11).

Like Honebein, Savery & Duffy (1996) attempt to link the theory of constructivism with the practice of instruction. They have derived a number of instructional principles from constructivism:

- Learning should be relevant.
- Instructional goals should be consistent with the learner's goals.
- Cognitive demands and tasks in the learning environment should be consistent with cognitive

demands and tasks for the environment for which the learner is being prepared.

- Instructors' role is to challenge the learners' thinking.
- Learners' ideas should be tested against alternate views through social negotiation and collaborative learning groups.
- Encourage reflection on the learning process (p. 137).

Many of the learning environments described in Wilson's book are based on similar principles. Wilson has organized these learning environments into three categories: computer microworlds, classroom-based learning environments and open, virtual environments. In the category of computer microworlds is the simulated work environment for specialized, avionics, electronics, maintenance training called *Sherlock*. The training system is an intelligent tutoring system designed to "accelerate the development of complex, technical problem skills" (p. 37). It provides extensive practice with coaching through a series of authentic problems which are an extension of learners' actual working environment and which operate at "the highest levels of real world difficulty". An essential part of *Sherlock* are "the tools for post-performance reflection" or the opportunities the environment provides for the learner to review a record of her problem-solving activity.

In the category of classroom-based learning environments, is a collaborative problem-solving project using the "Jasper" videodisc series as designed by the Cognition and Technology Group at Vanderbilt. The project was completed in the context of a research study by Young, Nastasi and Braunhardt who served each as instructor and researcher for the study. During a period of three months, a group of fifth grade learners were involved in a "complex, realistic problem-solving situation" using interactive videodisc technology and telecommunications. Although the specific focus of the problem-solving was in the area of mathematics, the content of the problems also involved other areas such as science, reading, writing, physical education and geography. During the course of the project, the learners solved three problems which required planning, information finding and cooperative group problem-solving.

The project was described as an experiment in "situated learning" or "situated cognition". By "situated" is meant "co-determined by the attributes of the context along with the attributes of the people involved" (p. 121). For this reason, considerable attention was paid to social interactions as well as academic behaviours. An important role of the instructors was to manage and guide the interactions among the groups of learners.

While collaboration is an important aspect of the situated learning project, it becomes the primary focus in the *CoVis Project* which Wilson has included in the category of open, virtual learning environments. *CoVis* or *Learning Through Collaborative Visualization Project* is described as "an integrated software environment that incorporates visualization tools for open-ended scientific investigations and communication tools for both synchronous and asynchronous collaboration" (p. 161). Participating high school learners are involved in authentic scientific practice using modified versions of scientists' tools in a social context including learners, instructors and scientists. Communication and collaboration are the central components of the philosophy behind the project. Learning is enhanced by communication with learner interactions and conversations resulting in new knowledge, reorganized knowledge or additional understanding. As well, learners are provided with the opportunity to communicate and develop relationships with practicing scientists.

Classrooms are equipped with computer workstations supporting high-speed video and a data network over ISDN, digital phone lines. E-mail, Usenet groups, Gopher, desktop video-conferencing, remote screen sharing and a collaborative notebook are some of the tools learners can access as part of the project. The primary component of the project is three scientific visualization environments covering three aspects of atmospheric science. Learners can access and manipulate data, generate questions, develop plans for identifying and exploring data as well as create artifacts to demonstrate their findings. Throughout the entire process, learners can collaborate and communicate with each other and with scientists to share concepts and viewpoints and to pose questions.

Discussion

In spite of the fact that constructivism is not a model of learning, it can provide a strong and coherent theory or set of principles which can serve as a guide in the design of learning environments. The many projects described in Wilson's book and the three projects summarized in this paper serve as specific examples of successful attempts at developing and implementing constructivist learning environments. Many of the environments exhibited common traits such as the authentic context for learning, collaborative work and an emphasis on problem-solving. The environments all relied on technology to facilitate the approach indicating that computers and related technology have an essential role to play in the realization of constructivist learning.

While it is encouraging to remark the large number of projects supporting constructivist principles of learning, the optimism must be tempered by the realization that these projects represent, not the norm in teaching and learning, but a departure from the norm. In this sense, the attempts to create constructivist learning environments are not yet part of the regular teaching practices of even a minority of instructors. On the contrary, these projects represent work carried out in the context of research projects which indicates that attempts at promoting constructivist learning are still at the research, experimental stage.

Wilson's book is important in that it moves the discussion of constructivism away from the philosophical and epistemological level to a more practical level of implementation. No doubt, there need to be more such attempts as this. Constructivism will remain an elusive ideal, and no more than theoretical fodder for philosophers and educational researchers unless there are concrete attempts at using the theory to create new approaches to teaching and learning. Increased access by schools to state-of-the-art technology should facilitate attempts to promote more authentic and collaborative learning environments in particular and constructivist learning environments in general. Constructivism, as a philosophy and theory of learning covers a set of principles that are broad enough to allow for great flexibility in implementation. This flexibility makes it accessible not only by designers but, as well, by classroom instructors interested in experimenting with a new approach to teaching and learning.

References

1. Cunningham, D., Duffy, T.M. and Knuth, R. (1993). Textbook of the future. In C. McKnight (Ed.), *Hypertext: A psychological perspective*. London: Ellis Horwood Publishing.
2. Honebein, P. (1996). Seven goals for the design of constructivist learning environments. In B. Wilson (Ed.), *Constructivist learning environments: Case studies in instructional design* (pp. 11-24). New Jersey: Educational Technology Publications.
3. Riesbeck, C. (1996). Case-based teaching and constructivism: Carpenters and tools. In B. Wilson (Ed.), *Constructivist learning environments: Case studies in instructional design* (pp. 49-61). New Jersey: Educational Technology Publications.
4. Savery, J. & Duffy, T. (1996). Problem-based learning: An instructional model and its constructivist framework. In B. Wilson (Ed.), *Constructivist learning environments: Case studies in instructional design* (pp. 135-48). New Jersey: Educational Technology Publications.
5. Wilson, B. (Ed.) (1996). *Constructivist learning environments: Case studies in instructional design*. New Jersey: Educational Technology Publications.
6. Young, M., Nastasi, B., Braunhardt, L. (1996). Implementing Jasper Immersion: A Case of Conceptual Change. In B. Wilson (Ed.), *Constructivist learning environments: Case studies in instructional design* (pp. 121-33). New Jersey: Educational Technology Publications.

This page was produced by Elizabeth Murphy in the context of courses TEN-61937 & TEN-61938, Université Laval, Québec City, Québec, Canada, Summer, 1997 with Gilles Larin.

ACTION LEARNING

Action Learning is the approach that links the world of learning with the world of action through a reflective process within small cooperative learning groups known as 'action learning sets' (McGill & Beaty 1995). The 'sets' meet regularly to work on individual members' real-life issues with the aim of learning with and from each other. The 'father' of Action Learning, Reg Revans, has said that there can be no learning without action and no (sober and deliberate) action without learning. Revans argued that learning can be shown by the following equation, where L is learning; P is programmed knowledge (e.g. traditional instruction) and Q is questioning insight. $L = P + Q$

Revans, along with many others who have used, researched and taught about this approach, argued that Action Learning is ideal for finding solutions to problems that do not have a 'right' answer because the necessary questioning insight can be facilitated by people learning with and from each other in action learning 'sets'.

Adult Learning

Malcolm Knowles (1978, 1990) is the theorist who brought the concept of adult learning to the fore. He has argued that adulthood has arrived when people behave in adult ways and believe themselves to be adults. Then they should be treated as adults. He taught that adult learning was special in a number of ways. For example:

- Adult learners bring a great deal of experience to the learning environment. Educators can use this as a resource.
- Adults expect to have a high degree of influence on what they are to be educated for, and how they are to be educated.
- The active participation of learners should be encouraged in designing and implementing educational programs.
- Adults need to be able to see applications for new learning.

- Adult learners expect to have a high degree of influence on how learning will be evaluated.
- Adults expect their responses to be acted upon when asked for feedback on the progress of the program.

Here is a quote from Burns (1995, p. 233). By adulthood people are self-directing. This is the concept that lies at the heart of adult learning and it is therefore learner-centered, experience-based, problem-oriented and collaborative very much in the spirit of the humanist approach to learning and education . . . the whole educational activity turns on the learner.

ADULTHOOD AS A SOCIAL CONSTRUCTION

Pogson and Tennant (1995) provide a perspective of adulthood as a social structure. They say that the concept of a life's path varies for different individuals and different cultures; therefore trainers and adult educators should be wary of definitive views of adults and their behaviour.

Burns would probably support this view as he discusses the notion that "definitions of the adult are not clear" and says "the same is true of adult education". He discusses the 'petrol tank' view of school education: 'fill the tank full at the only garage before the throughway, then away we go on life's journey' (1995, p. 227). He goes on to discuss that problems can arise when people have not had their tank filled completely at school and he extends the metaphor to suggest that there should be service stations along 'the length of the highway of life'.

The question could be asked—when is maturity complete? Is there no further development after a certain stage in life? Some authors think that while children at approximately the same age are at the same stage of development, the same cannot be said of adults. Adults would vary in levels of awareness and also in their life experiences. There could be said to be tremendous variation in adult experience.

An Adult's Emotional Response can Affect Learning

Some adults can approach formal educational settings with anxiety and feelings of high or low self-efficacy. Their approach to new learning contexts can be influenced by how they appraise or estimate the new experience.

Let's assume two adults in a classroom where an exercise is about to begin, one individual may interpret the exercise in such a way that leads to a feeling of 'excitement', while the other person interprets the exercise in such a way that leads to the feeling of 'embarrassment'. It is self evident that the way the individual interprets the circumstances and the subsequent emotion that arises, will affect the kind of action the individual is to take. (Burns, 1995, p. 16)

Burns considers that such evaluations, coupled with labels such as 'fear' or 'anxiety' can lead some learners to perceptively get out from the source of humiliation that is the learning experience. However, when coupled with labels such as pleasure or 'challenge' the learner is led to take actions that focus on the task.

Theories and theorists all have provided different concepts about adult learning and with experience educators have developed various models and have given shape to the research in the area of learning and we educators must understand the reasons why adults go to school or college. Various reasons have been discussed and shared in faculty development programs few of them are as follows:

- Adults go to school for fulfilling a dream
- Get a job or promotion
- Change careers
- For achieving social satisfaction
- For gaining expertise
- To compete with the peer pressure

Researchers have mentioned that adults develop their learning process in various ways in comparison to young learners and children. The learning process makes the concept clear and that lasts the entire life of each individual, it also allows an individual to acquire, renew, upgrade, or complete knowledge, skills, and attitudes for functioning effectively in a constantly changing society.

Malcolm Knowles have developed a model based on following assumptions:

- Adults need to know why they are learning
- Adults want to be seen as competent
- Adults need to be self-directed and experientially involved in their learning
- Adults want learning to be life-centered and applicable
- Adults do not learn for the sheer pleasure of learning

As we all know compared to children, and teens, adults have special needs and requirements as learners. Despite the apparent truth, adult learning is a relatively new area of study. Malcolm has identified the following characteristics of adult learners:

- Adults are *autonomous* and *self-directed*: It is observed that adults need to be free to direct themselves. Their instructors must actively involve adult participants in the learning process and serve as facilitators for them. Specifically, they must get participant's perspectives about what topics to cover and let them work on projects that reflect their interests. They should allow the participants to assume responsibility for presentations and group leaders.
- Adults are *goal-oriented*: Upon enrolling in a course, they usually know what goal they want to attain. They, therefore, appreciate and education program that is organized and has clearly defined elements. Instructors must show participants how this class will help them achieve their goals. This classification of goals and course objectives must be done early in the course.
- Adults have accumulated a foundation of *life experiences* and knowledge that may include work-related activities, family responsibilities, and previous education. They need to connect learning to this knowledge/experience base. To help them do so, they should draw out participants experience and knowledge which is relevant to the topic. They must relate theories and concepts to the participants and recognize the value of experience in learning.
- Adults are *relevancy-oriented*. They must see a reason for learning something. Learning has to be applicable

to their work or other responsibilities to be of value to them. Therefore, instructors must identify objectives for adult participants before the course begins. This means, also that theories and concepts must be related to setting familiar to participants. This need can be fulfilled by letting participants choose projects that reflect their own interests.

- Adults are *practical,* focusing on the aspects of a lesson most useful to them in their work. They may not be interested in knowledge for its own sake. Instructors must tell participants explicitly how the lesson will be useful to them on the job.

Barriers and Motivation

Adults have many responsibilities that they must balance against the demands of learning. Due to these responsibilities, adults have *barriers against participating in learning*. These barriers include lack of time management, money, confidence, lack of information about opportunities to learn, scheduling problems, "administrative as well as political red tape," and problems with child care system, (which exists in the west but is still invisible in most of Asian countries including India) and transportation.

Motivation factors differ from person to person and from one age group to another. Motivation factors sometimes take shape of a barrier. What motivates adult learners is different in comparison to toddlers and teenagers. It is normally observed that the best way to motivate adult learners is simply to *enhance* their reasons for enrolling and *decrease* the barriers. Instructors must learn why their learners are enrolled; they have to discover what is keeping them from learning. Then the instructors must plan their motivating strategies.

Learning Tips for Effective Instructors

Instructors must remember that learning occurs within each creature as a continual process throughout life. People learn at dissimilar speeds, so it is natural for them to be impatient or nervous when faced with a learning situation. Positive corroboration by the instructor can enhance learning, as can proper timing of the instruction. In some people, one sense is used more than others to learn or recall information. Instructors should present materials that stimulate as many senses as possible in order to increase their chances of teaching success.

There are four critical elements of learning that must be addressed to ensure that participants learn. These elements are.

1. motivation
2. reinforcement
3. retention
4. transference

Motivation—If the participant does not recognize the need for the information, all of the instructor's effort to assist the participant to learn will be futile. The instructor must establish rapport with participants and prepare them for learning; this provides motivation. Instructors can motivate learners via several means:

- *Set a feeling or tone for the lesson*—Instructors should try to establish a friendly, open environment that shows the participants they will facilitate them learn.
- *Set an appropriate level of concern*—The level of tension must be adjusted to meet the level of importance of the objective. If the material has a high level of importance, a higher level of tension/stress should be established in the class. However, people learn best under low to moderate stress; if the stress is too high, it becomes a barrier to learning.

- *Set an appropriate level of difficulty*—The degree of difficulty should be set high enough to challenge participants but not so high that they become frustrated by information overload. The instruction should predict and reward participation, culminating in success.

In addition, participants need specific knowledge of their learning results and that is normally designed as feedback. Feedback must be specific, not general and this helps learners in feeling the reward for learning. The reward does not necessarily have to be financial; it can be simply a manifestation of benefits to be realized from learning the material. Finally, the participant must be *interested* in the subject and this interest is directly related to benefit. Adults must see the benefit of learning in order to motivate them to learn the subject.

Reinforcement—Reinforcement is a very necessary part of the coaching/learning process; through it, instructors encourage correct modes of behavior and performance.

- *Positive reinforcement* is normally used by instructors who are teaching participants new skills. As the name implies, positive corroboration is "good" and reinforces "good" behavior.
- *Negative reinforcement* is usually used by instructors teaching a new skill or new information. It is useful in trying to change modes of behavior. The result of negative reinforcement is *extinction,* i.e., the instructor uses negative reinforcement until the "bad" behavior disappears, or it becomes extinct.

Reinforcement should be part of the teaching and learning process to make sure correct conduct. Instructors need to use it on a recurrent and regular basis early in the process to help the learners retain what they have learned. Then, they should use reinforcement only to preserve consistent, positive behavior.

Retention—Learners must retain information from classes in order to benefit from the learning. The instructors' jobs are not finished until they have assisted the learner in retaining the information. In order for participants to retain the information taught, they must see a meaning or purpose for that information. They must also understand and be able to construe and apply the information. This understanding includes their ability to assign the correct degree of importance to the material.

Retention by the participants is directly affected by their amount of practice during the learning. Instructors should emphasize retention and application. After the learners demonstrate correct performance, they should be urged to practice to maintain the desired performance.

Transference—Transfer of learning is the result of training—it is the ability to use the information taught in the course but in a new setting. As with reinforcement, there are two types of transfer: *positive* and *negative*.

- Positive transference, like positive reinforcement, occurs when the participants uses the behavior taught in the course.
- Negative transference, again like negative reinforcement, occurs when the participants do not do what they are told not to do.

Transference is most likely to occur in the following situations:

- Association—participants can associate the new information with something that they already know.
- Similarity—the information is similar to material that participants already know; that is, it revisits a logical framework or pattern.
- Degree of original learning—participant's degree of original learning was high.
- Critical attribute element—the information learned contains elements that are extremely beneficial on the job.

Although adult learning is relatively new as field of study, it is just as substantial as traditional education and carries, potential for greater achievement. The heightened success requires a greater accountability on the part of the instructor. Additionally, the learners come to the course with precisely defined expectations. Unfortunately, there are barriers to their learning and the best motivators for adult learners are significance and selfish benefit. If they can be shown that the course benefits them pragmatically, they will perform better, and the benefits will be longer lasting.

4

Learner Support Services

Educators as well as learners have to agree with us that education, whether it is part of continuing education or not, is dependent upon two-way communication. India and most of the Asian countries believe in pumping or we should say assimilating information, whereas the educators from the developed world have realized that simply accessing or assimilating information is not sufficient. In modern day's education there is growing call for, and admiration of, continuous two-way communication in the route of analyzing and developing knowledge. Meeting the demands of an education transaction is dependent upon communication technologies which provide frequent and regular communication between instructor and learning, as well as

among learners. The focus of much institutional effort has been directed toward delivery of knowledge for the learner and nature of human-to-human and human-to-machine interactions in the learning process.

In today's education system, we the educators must accept the reality that as instructors we are providing service to our learners and learners are no where less than our clients. Client satisfaction is most important and education systems are taking shape of industry which is totally dependent upon the customers for survival. With the mushrooming of universities, government universities, deemed to be universities, private universities and private institutes, somewhere down the line the importance and respect for education and teaching community is being diluted. Customer is the king-maker and now we are able to see that learners are actively involved in giving direction to the academic institutes where they study.

Learner support services play an active role in making two-way communication possible, the term 'learner support' means the range of activities which harmonize the mass produced materials which make up of the most well-known learning tool. Tutoring and counseling are considered as complementary but necessary services, interacting teaching through television, and radio and other similar activities are also being used in upcoming institutions.

WHAT ARE SUPPORT SERVICES?

A range of services are provided through activities such as:

- Language support
- Career guidance
- Administrative problem-solving
- Peer group support
- Tutoring individually and in groups
- Advice/counseling

Robinson (1995) has viewed learner support as having three components: the elements that make up the system, their configuration, and the interaction between them and the learners, which creates its dynamics. The elements of the system are:

- Peer contact;
- Access to libraries, laboratories, equipment, and communication networks;
- Additional materials such as handbook, advice noted or guides;
- Personal contact between learners, individuals or groups, face-to-face or via other means;
- Case study, group work; and
- Presentations.

Arrangement of these elements varies, depending on the requirements of course design, infrastructure of a country, distribution of learners, available resources, and the values and philosophy of the education provider. Information technology has given a new dimension to the concept of learner support. The regard for face-to-face interaction, as deliberately advanced to all other forms of interaction, will be overcome with the pervasive use of new information and communication technologies. Electronic media has transformed the instructional methods it can also transform the method of providing support to learners.

Types of Electronic Learning Support

General Information	Web Pages Home Pages Bulletin Boards Interactive Voice Response System (IVRS)
Pre-admission Counseling	IVRS E-mail Bulletin Boards
Course Content	CD-ROM On-line Hyperlink to other Websites
Counseling/tutoring	E-mail IVRS Conferencing Chat sessions
Projects/Assignments	On- Line
Group Discussion	Conferencing

NEED FOR SUPPORT SERVICES

Learner support services appear important in continuing education as well as professional development programmes, because of the special characteristics of this system of learning. When the learners join any academic programme they find themselves in an unfamiliar situation. Learners normally associate learning with being taught by an instructor who is physically as well as mentally present while delivering lecture. But, now they will be expected to learn for a good proportion of their time on their own, in the absence of an instructor. Adult education is bit different and learners are also different in comparison to fresh school leavers who enter colleges, institutes and universities. Many adult learners are not generally confident of their capacity to learn through unfamiliar learning material and they sometimes feel threatened by overload of text. For adults learning might be a disorienting experience, not only for fresh learners doing basic courses, but also for experienced, who may have gained their qualifications through more conservative routes.

CHARACTERISTICS OF PROFESSIONAL DEVELOPMENT LEARNERS

We have seen lot of comparisons between different kinds of teaching styles and different kinds of learners and we do have some basic understanding about the differences between conventional system and distance education system. As we know conventional learner belongs to an institution, but a distance learner is a member of many institutions, most of which (e.g. work, family, etc.) take precedence over the institution which provides his/her courses. In conventional system, the learner is in easy contact with the institution, however, in the continuing education system the learner might be isolated, as contact with university/institution is infrequent and often takes place across a distance.

Conventional System	*Professional Development—Continuing Education System*
• Learning is a full time and major activity • The learner 'belongs' to an institution • The learner is usually young • The learner is in easy contact with the fellow learners • The learner has easy access to institutional resources • Learning is a part-time secondary activity	• The learner is a member of many institutions (e.g. work, family), most of which take precedence over the learning process • Contact between fellow learners may not be easy • The learner is most of the time an adult • The learner's contact with the academic body is infrequent and often takes place across a distance.

As noted, a learner in the conventional system has to attend classes on a full time basis unlike his/her counterpart in the continuing education system, who needs to devote only a part of his/her time to his/her studies. Continuing learners, who are mostly adults, have responsibilities towards their job, family and other commitments.

In words of Koul (1989), generally we find three categories of learners in continuing learning system. The first category is that of learners who have confidence in their ability to work on their own. They are confident enough to think that they can succeed without any guidance from the counselor. They are the opens who may not make any contact with the counselors thought-out the programme. However, it should be remembered that simply having or feeling confidence in their ability to succeed without the help of a counselor need not necessarily lead to success. Many of them, in spite of being very sure of their abilities may finally need help. The help should therefore, available for them as well.

The second category of learners are the ones who actually need talking to. Having somebody help in solving their problems gives them reassurance about the system as well as builds a little more confidence in them. For them, a face-to-face support system can make all the difference between retreating from the course and finishing it.

The third category of learners, who fall between the above two types, are the ones who are really sitting out of the playground. If only they run into intractable problems they approach the counselor for help.

SCHOLASTIC SOCIALIZATION

Open and distance learning is different from correspondence study and teach yourself programme, systematic efforts need to be made to orient the new entrants into the system. Continuing education learners are mostly adult learners, and the usefulness of adult learning varies with learning ability, but is also affected by the approach the adult takes to the learning activity. It would ideal for continuing education departments to organize induction programmes for their new entrants as these programmes are designed to assist learners in ways which are listed below:

- Develop a sense of identification with the institution and familiarize them with its functioning;
- Introduce them particularly to the instructional package and delivery system;
- Help in their transition to life as tertiary learner particularly as continuing education learners;
- Introduce them with self-directed motivational learning method and thereby structuring goal autonomy and individual accountability;
- Motivate, encourage learner by using local environment; and
- Help minimize a number of post-entry problems reducing the dropout rate.

Induction into the system is very essential as it prepares the learner for his/her intellectual socialization with learning methods and contributes to his/her preparation for learning.

There is not set pattern of learner support in professional development as well as continuing education. The nature of learner support services varies from institution to institution and from one instructor to another. Among professional development educators there are basically two different approaches to learner support; one relying entirely on non-contiguous communication. Basic difference is that—although it does not completely coincide with other doctrines: there are two distinct types of learners, those taking the odd course to appendage their education and those who study at a distance to acquire degree or a similar measure of proficiency.

READING SKILLS

In Indian context, there is virtually no systematic teaching of reading skills either at the lower or higher levels of education. Subsequent on this, learners suffer considerably at advanced levels. Many of us are aware of the value attached to reading; and some of us tend to ignore the significance of teaching reading systematically. The primary reason for such attitudes, perhaps, is our naïve concept of 'reading'. Different studies of learning theories have also shown that learners retain information over an extended period of time, if they are able to relate what they are reading to the materials which they have already read several times.

Learners are active consumers of information must have strategies to process, absorb and understandably accommodate information. Learner should be able to relate new experiences to what they already know and they must accept the fact that no one can do this for the reader. Instructor can help facilitate reading and the instruction and putting together of meaning but cannot force assimilation of information in any learners mind.

Learning process is correlated with different aspects of learning and acquiring skills and the importance of reading skills for a toddler's success cannot be emphasized enough. Learning is based on the interest as well as understanding of individual learner and we all know that importance of reading skills filters into all aspects of learning. Many parents are of the opinion that importance of reading skills is only evident in language arts, they are all entitled to have any opinion, but reality is different. We must comprehend that those who don't have adequate reading skills, they won't ever be able to succeed in language arts and they'll suffer and stumble in other areas of academic and professional competence, as well. Let's move ahead and take a look at social studies, for gaining further insight into this idea let's take a close look at social studies. Whether your child is learning about his neighborhood in nursery, or learning about other countries and continents in the fifth grade, he or she needs to be able to read in order to have a rich learning experience. Map reading and other basics of social studies; emphasize the importance of reading skills.

Speed Reading

Radically Increasing Your Reading Speed

Speed Reading can help you to read and understand written information much more quickly. This makes it an essential skill in any environment where you have to master large volumes of information quickly, as is the norm in fast-moving professional environments. What's more, it's a key technique to learn if you suffer from "information overload", because it helps you to become much more discriminating about the information that you consume.

The Key Insight

The most important trick about speed reading is to know what information you want from a document before you start reading it. If you only want an outline of the issue that the document discusses, then you can skim the document quickly and extract only the essential facts. If you need to understand the real detail of the document, then you need to read it slowly enough to gain the full understanding you need.

You will get the greatest time savings from speed reading by learning to skim excessively detailed documents, although the techniques you'll learn will help you improve the speed of all the reading you do.

Technical Issues

Even when you know how to ignore irrelevant detail, there are other technical improvements you can make to your reading style which will increase your reading speed.

Most people learn to read the way young children read—either letter-by-letter, or word-by-word. As an adult, this is probably not the way you read now: Just think about how your eye muscles are moving as you read this. You will probably find that you are fixing your eyes on one block of words, then moving your eyes to the next block of words, and so on. You are reading blocks of words at a time, not individual words one-by-one. You may also notice that you do not always go from one block to the next: sometimes you may move back to a previous block if you are unsure about something.

A skilled reader will read many words in each block. He or she will only dwell on each block for an instant, and will then move on. Only rarely will the reader's eyes skip back to a previous block of words. This reduces the amount of work that the reader's eyes have to do. It also increases the volume of information that can be assimilated in a given period of time.

A poor reader will become bogged down, spending a lot of time reading small blocks of words. He or she will skip back often, losing the flow and structure of the text, and confusing his or her overall understanding of the subject. This irregular eye movement makes reading tiring. Poor readers tend to dislike reading, and they may find it harder to concentrate, and understand written information.

How to Use Tool

Speed reading aims to improve reading skills by:

- Increasing the number of words read in each block.
- Reducing the length of time spent reading each block.
- And reducing the number of times your eyes skip back to a previous sentence.

These are explained below:

Increasing the number of words in each block

This needs a conscious effort. Try to expand the number of words that you read at a time: With practice, you'll find you read faster. You may also find that you can increase the number of words in each block by holding the text a little further from your eyes. The more words you can read in each block, the faster you will read!

Reducing fixation time

The minimum length of time needed to read each block is probably only a quarter of a second. By pushing yourself to reduce the time you take, you will get better at picking up information quickly. Again, this is a matter of practice and confidence.

Reducing skip-back

To reduce the number of times that your eyes skip back to a previous sentence, run a pointer along the line as you read. This could be a finger, or a pen or pencil. Your eyes will follow the tip of your pointer, smoothing the flow of your reading. The speed at which you read using this method will largely depend on the speed at which you move the pointer.

You will be able to increase your reading speed a certain amount on your own by applying these speed reading techniques.

What you don't get out of self-study is the use of specialist reading machines and the confidence gained from successful speed-reading—this is where a good one-day course can revolutionize your reading skills.

Key points: By speed reading you can read information more quickly. You may also get a better understanding of it, as you will hold more of it in short-term memory.

To improve the speed of your reading, read more words in each block and reduce the length of time spent reading each block. Use a pointer to smooth the way your eyes move and reduce skip-back.

As an instructor and as a parent we must accept the different learning and teaching styles, if your learner does not have basic sound-symbol recognition skills, he/she will have a terrible time finding Israel. If, however your learner does have these skills, he/she will know that the country he/she is looking for starts with letter I and has the letters E and L in it. With this knowledge, the learner has a greater chance of locating the country successfully.

If the learner has solid reading skills, then the learner will be able to successfully follow the theoretical procedures and if the learner lacks in these skills then might lead towards the negative side. Failure in academic as well as professional development might be frustrating and disappointing for any learner. It can even result your learner disliking academic work, because he/she sees it as a task in which he/she can't be successful.

Now-a-days, more emphasis is being placed on the problem solving aspects, therefore even subjects like mathematics includes many story problems, which require reading and comprehension skills. An individual learner with a strong mathematical mind, but poor reading skills, can't possibly do well in today's mathematics, statistics and operational research classes. The importance of reading skills is so high that it is nearly impossible to understand and successfully get credits for mathematics without being able to read and comprehend intelligently.

How to Improve Reading Skills
Teaching Fluency and Comprehension Skills to Enhance Reading-Jennifer Wagaman

Use these strategies to improve reading fluency and comprehension in children who struggle in reading.

During the primary school years, grades K-3, children learn how to read. Starting in grade 4, children begin to read to learn. This is often the age when reading grades start to slip, comprehension becomes an issue and instructors are often commenting to parents that their child needs additional support in the area of reading.

Improve Reading Fluency

The best way to help a child to read fluently is to simply have him read frequently. Instructors should require 30 minutes of reading per day for each child. A non-reader (a child who cannot read), can repeat lines that the parent reads to learn inflection and phrasing, and can listen to stories read to him.

Young readers can share the reading with the parent, switching every page or every paragraph or even every sentence. Re-reading books over again is another great strategy that will help teach expression and reading in phrases. The child should learn to pause at the end of sentences and put the correct inflection in his voice for exclamation points and question marks. A young fluent reader should be encouraged to read a variety of books and can read to a younger sibling.

Improve Reading Comprehension

There are three basic strategies that when used can help improve a child's reading comprehension.

Before Reading Strategies

"Before reading" activities happen before reading a new

book. Have the child predict what the book is about by looking at the front cover and doing a picture walk through the book. A picture walk is "walking" through the book, looking at pictures and talking about what is happening without reading the words. Guide young children to use basic logic skills while looking at the pictures to form an idea of what the story will be about. This will help hone prediction skills and will give them a set of ideas about the story that they can use to help decode any unfamiliar words they come across while reading.

During Reading Strategies

"During reading" activities happen while reading the actual text. Ask questions while reading the book. Questions can be as simple as "what did she say?" requiring simple recall, or as difficult as "why did she say that?" requiring an inference. Make sure children understand what is going on in the story and ask them what they think will happen next before turning the page. When asking a difficult question, show the children how to find the answer by re-reading a part of the story.

After Reading Strategies

"After reading" activities occur after you have finished reading the story. See if the children can explain what happened at the beginning, in the middle and at the end of the story. Have them identify the characters, the setting, the plot and the solution. Ask who, what, where, when, how and why questions. These questions should be appropriately tailored to each age group. Ask how the characters felt when something specific happened in the story, requiring the children to infer and connect to the text. Encourage them to look back in the story for answers they cannot remember and show them how to do so.

Reading is only half the battle when it comes to comprehension. Engaging children in the story will pay-off in greater comprehension of what they are reading. The more a child practices reading to improve fluency and comprehension, the better readers he will become.

Reading can be loosely defined as the ability to make sense of written words. It is observed that the reader uses the symbols to activate the information from his/her memory and afterward uses this information to disembark at a credible understanding of the writer's message. For most people reading is an automatic process and there is rarely any occasion for them to pause for a minute and consider what the process entails. It is known that a skilled reader is generally able to identify any one of the words in his/her repertoire in a fraction of a second. Any learner can do this, despite the fact that the constituent letters are frequently represented by different shapes from one text to another—in the case of handwriting, from one instance of the letter to the other. Learner can even think and identify the words which have been misprinted.

Trying Reading this—

p??u??ds?? u??q ???? ????? sp?o? ??? ????u?p? pu? ?u??? u??? u?? ??u???l ÿ????o ??? o? ?????l ??? ?o ??u??su? ?uo ?o?? ??u?????pu?? ?o ?s?? ??? u? ????ou? o? ?x?? ?uo ?o?? s?d??s ?u??????p ?q p??u?s??d?? ?l?u?nb??? ??? s?????l ?u?n???suo? ??? ???? ???? ??? ???ds?p ?s??? op u?? ??u???l ?u? ÿpuo??s ? ?o uo?????? ? u? ???o???d?? ???/s?? u? sp?o? ??? ?o ?uo ?u? ????u?p? o? ?lq? ?ll???u?? s? ??p??? p?ll??s ? ???? u?ou? s? ?? ÿɔl???u? ss??o?d ??? ???? ??p?suo? pu? ??nu?? ? ?o? ?sn?d o? ???? ?o? uo?s???o ?u? ?l???? s? ????? pu? ss??o?d ?????o?u? u? s? ?u?p??? ?ldo?d ?so? ?o? ÿ???ss?? s,?????? ??? ?o ?u?pu??s??pun ?lq?p??? ? ?? ???q??s?p o? uo?????o?u? s??? s?sn p???????? pu? ??o??? ???/s?? ?o?? uo?????o?u? ??? ???????? o? sloq??s ??? s?sn ??p??? ??? ???? p????sqo s? ?? ÿsp?o? u?????? ?o ?su?s ???? o? ???l?q? ??? s? p?u???p ?l?sool ?q u?? ?u?p???

Accomplished readers can thus cope with fact that many words have different meaning in different contexts. They can use this knowledge to unfold haziness and appreciate prevarications. Knowledgeable learners can combine meanings of individual words to derive meanings of sentences and more extended passages of prose and poetry. Individual learner may involve in drawing inferences, recalling pertinent experiences, constructing images of scenes, and appreciating shades of meaning. After considering the fact that reading involves a number of processes, we cannot be content with the statement that reading is to decode printed or written words.

Defining Reading

Finding a single definition for reading might be a cumbersome task for any researcher. Schoenbach, Greenleaf, Cziko, and Hurwitz (1999) define reading as a complex process that is situationally bounded. They explain that fluent reading is not the same as accurate decoding. Fluent reading occurs as the reader interactively relates to the text in order to gain connotation, increase knowledge, and achieve reading expertise. The experiences readers bring to the content impact their level of proficiency. For example, a learner who has no problem reading a short story may be much less proficient at reading a political essay. This is due to the fact that reading proficiency does not extend to all texts for all readers. Reading involves problem-solving, and some readers are more proficient within an explicit genre or type of text while others have talent across various types of texts. However, these readers do share a common set of characteristics. As proficient readers, they are psychologically engaged, aggravated, and strategic.

Wilhelm, Baker, and Dube (2001) present literacy as strategic reading that is teaching- and learning-centered. Based on a socio-cultural model, learning is dependent upon a learner's interactions with the instructors and others. The instructor's role involves scaffolding learning within both small-group and whole-class learning. Literacy coaching includes modeling and guided practice that makes the use of reading strategies visible to learners. Instructors are explicit as they make these strategies available to learners. Learners then have opportunities to practice as instructors take the role of participant observers. While literacy learning is a joint effort between learners and instructors, it is the instructor's responsibility to monitor and adjust instruction to insure learner progress. As per Wikipedia—*Reading (process)* is the human cognitive process of decoding symbols or syntax for the purpose of deriving meaning (reading comprehension) or constructing meaning.

A look at the range of reading styles will show the inadequacy of definitions, such as, 'reading is the identification of written words' or 'reading is the appreciation of the author's thoughts'. A broad definition that has been extensively used and accepted is that reading is a route whereby a reader brings meaning to and gets meaning from print. This implies that readers bring their backgrounds, their experiences, as well as their emotions into play in order to derive meaning from a text. If we are in conversation with someone, we can stop him/her and ask for explanations whenever we need them.

To elaborate, the point that a writer wants to express does not merely lie in the text, waiting to be unreceptively absorbed by the reader. Instead the reader with his/her background and experience introduces meaning into the text so as to tailor it into comprehensive chunks to suit his/her purpose. Educators have long known that reading is an interactive process. It won't be wrong to define reading as a multifaceted and coated process in which a reader by actively interacting with the text, tries to decode what has been encoded by the author. Through reading the learner establishes a meaningful communication directly as well as indirectly with the author.

Teaching Reading Comprehension Skills

Educators differ and have different views on teaching reading comprehension skills. Comprehension in itself varies from person to person and reading in itself has no inherent, fixed subject matter, whatever the reader reads constitutes the practice of reading—whether the individual is reading a newspaper, book, journal, a road map, the efficiency of the individual learner reading depends upon the following:

- Basic reading skills,
- Experiences in the area in which learner is reading,
- Interest in the material,
- Purpose of reading, and
- Level of difficulty of the material.

An investigation roughly a decade ago revealed that forty to forty four million Americans had only the most basic reading and writing skills (*Kirsch, Jungeblut, Jenkins, & Kolstad, 1993*).

Almost fifty million Americans not only lacked the skills to function effectively in an educated society, but also were not receptive of their inadequacies. These statistics make it obvious that educators have to look for new approaches to prepare learners for the current job market trends. The job market now demands a personnel that is more highly educated than ever. Modern time's management expects, assembly line workers must be capable of interpreting manuals in addition to operating machines. It is expected that these workers must be able to read, write, analyze, interpret, and synthesize information and must be capable of multi-tasking also.

Educators and researchers know that people just aren't reading as much anymore and yet the need for reading, comprehension, and communication skills has increased. The need is great for strengthening the following skills:

- Your ability to understand and remember what you read.
- Your ability to read a variety of materials (e.g. textbooks, novels, newspapers, magazines, instructional manuals).
- Your ability to effectively communicate what you've learned from your reading.

According to Webster's Dictionary, comprehension is "the capacity for understanding fully; the act or action of grasping with the intellect." Webster also tells us that reading is "to receive or take in the sense of (as letters or symbols) by scanning; to understand the meaning of written or printed matter; to learn from what one has seen or found in writing or printing.

Comprehension thus is the ability for understanding those thoughts and ideas. When you comprehend what you read it like taking a trip around the world, staying as long as you like, visiting all the places you wish, and you never even have to pack a bag! All the learners must understand that they don't have to be a reader who reads without thinking or who reads without a purpose.

We all including educators and learners can become an active, effective reader through intellectual capacity. Learner must try master few skills of comprehension regulation; it is nothing but a method for consciously controlling the reading process. Comprehension regulation involves the use of preplanned strategies for gaining better understanding of the text. It is a plan for getting the most out of reading. It allows you to have an idea of what to expect from the text. As an active reader, you can get an idea of what the writer is trying to communicate by:

- Setting goals based on your purpose for reading
- Previewing the text to make predictions
- Self-questioning
- Scanning
- Relating new information to old

Although, reading means different things to different people and skills vary with every individual, reading is a skill that can be improved. Learners from various backgrounds are in reading courses for a variety of reasons. Weaknesses in vocabulary, comprehension, speed, or a combination of all three may be the result of ineffective reading habits. Active reading is engaged reading and can be achieved through comprehension regulation strategies.

How to Teach ESL Reading

When considering how to teach ESL reading skills to second language learners, the most important concept to convey is that reading, like writing, is a process. Strong readers don't just sit down with a text, read it once, and completely understand it. Whether readers are aware of it or not, they employ techniques like pre-reading and making predictions to connect the particular text they are presently reading with texts they have read before. For ESL students, scaffolding this process into distinct steps is an effective way to build reading comprehension.

Pre-reading

Getting ready to read is one of the most important parts of the reading process. Situating the text in terms of its genre and audience can help ESL students approach reading with a critical mindset. Before reading the assignment, ask students to think about the following questions to encourage them to construct a context for the reading:

- Where did the material come from? Is it an excerpt from a book, a magazine, an online article, or a journal? Knowing where the material being read comes from tells a great deal about how the piece of writing may be arranged and what its purpose is. An editorial is intended to persuade readers to believe what the author believes, whereas an article from a scholarly journal is typically written to inform.
- Who wrote the article? Do you know anything about the author? What other types of materials has he/she written? How could you find out more about the writer? Knowledge of who the author of the material is allows ESL students to enter into the conversation as active participants in the rhetorical process and not passive observers.
- What is the title of the piece? Can you determine

what the topic of the issue that will be discussed is from the title? What else has been written about this topic? What do you already know about the issue at hand? Having ESL students relate to readings through their existing knowledge system will inspire a more personal interaction between the reader and the text.

- Who are the intended readers? What does the writer know or assume about his/her audience? How does the author address this audience? Who might have a strong opinion about the topic the reading addresses? An understanding of audience allows ESL students a chance to better understand how writing functions to persuade, influence, entertain, or inform.

Make Predictions

Instructors will assist student comprehension by constructing questions about the reading for students to answer before they read the assigned text for the first time. Doing this helps students make predictions about the text and encourages critical interaction when they read. For example, if the students will be reading an article on animal rights, you may ask questions that help provide a background on the issue.

1. How many groups of people can you think of that have strong feelings about animals?
2. What are the feelings of these groups towards animals? How are they similar? How are they different?
3. What might cause someone to change how they feel about animals?
4. Judging by the title, what do you think the purpose of this article is?
5. The article first appeared in *People* magazine? Who do you think the audience is?

Introduce Vocabulary

ESL students often struggle to understand new words and phrases. Reading exercises are an ideal way for these students to expand their working vocabularies. Instructors should create a vocabulary list of important or challenging words from the reading to hand out. Students can look up the words in a dictionary and write down the definitions. This exercise encourages ESL students to both learn the meanings of new words and phrases and to apply those meanings to the understanding of the assigned text.

First Reading

Have the students read through the text one time. Their main purpose during the first reading is to achieve a working understanding of the text. After they finish reading, have them answer questions that connect the earlier steps of the reading process with their working understanding of the text.

1. Did any of your predictions about the text based on the title turn out to be true?
2. What, if anything, surprised you?
3. What is the author's purpose or argument? Is he/she trying to persuade, inform, describe, etc.?
4. What kinds of support are provided by the author to make his/her case?
5. Does the author want the readers to take an action of any kind?

Re-Reading

After developing a working understanding of the text, students should look for the author's claims and assertions and determine if s/he backs them up effectively. Also, look for stylistic choices the author makes and analyze them for their effectiveness.

- Highlight the major points of the writing. Note the thesis statement (the paper's main point) and the other major claims the author makes.

- Highlight the evidence and supporting information the author provides in a different color than you used to mark the major points.
- Mark up the text! Ask questions and write comments in the margins.
- What is the style of the article? Formal? Informal? Funny? Scholarly? Is it effective?

Final Thoughts

The above process of how to teach ESL reading skills can be extended in many different directions depending on the purpose of the assignment, the level of the student population, etc. Students could summarize the reading or respond to it by extending an aspect of the reading they found interesting. Instructors could also assign short answer questions that further encourage critical thinking or use the exercise as a starting point for a larger writing assignment.

FIND THE JOB THAT'S RIGHT FOR YOU!

1. Nearly 50% of all workers in the United States have jobs they aren't happy with. Don't let this happen to you! If you want to find the right job, don't rush to look through the classified ads in the newspaper. Instead, sit down and think about yourself. What kind of person are you? What makes you happy?
2. According to psychologist John Holland, there are six types of personalities. Nobody is just one personality type, but most

- The *Realistic* is practical and likes working with machines and tools.
- The *Investigative* type is curious and likes to learn, analyze situations, and solve problems.
- The *Artistic* type is imaginative and likes to express himself or herself by creating art.
- The *Social* type is friendly and likes helping or training other people.
- The *Enterprising* type is outgoing and likes to persuade or lead other people.

people are mainly one type. For each type, there are certain jobs that might be right and others that are probably wrong.

3. Considering your personality type can help you make the right job decision. Yue Yanting is a good example. Yue knew she could help children as a school counselor or instructor. She took counseling and teaching courses—and hated them. After talking to a career counselor, she realized the problem was that she's an Artistic type. Yue studied film, and she now produces children's TV shows and loves it.

- The *Conventional* type is careful and likes to follow routines and keep track of details.

A. *Read the article. Then find these sentences in the article. Decide whether each sentence is the main idea or a supporting idea in that paragraph. Circle the ideas and then tell with they fell in main idea category or in supporting idea category.*

	Main Idea	*Supporting Idea*
1. Nearly 50% of all workers .....they aren't happy.		
2. According to psychologist ....types of personalities.		
3. For each type, there are ...that are probably wrong.		
4. Considering your personality ...the right job decision.		
5. After talking to a career counselor...an Artistic type.		

B. For each personality type, write two examples of appropriate jobs. Then explain your answers to a partner.

Realistic	*Investigative*	*Artistic*	*Social*	*Enterprising*	*Conventional*

C. *Group Work*—What personality type do you think you are? Does your group agree?

5 Teaching Techniques

Teaching as we know is more than a way of enhancing knowledge and giving back to the society. Teaching and instructors have been in existence since the beginning of the systems of education. Instructors at different levels have different teaching techniques which they use from time to time and change the techniques depending upon the level of learners and the academic environment where they have been teaching. We instructors have realized the importance of words in

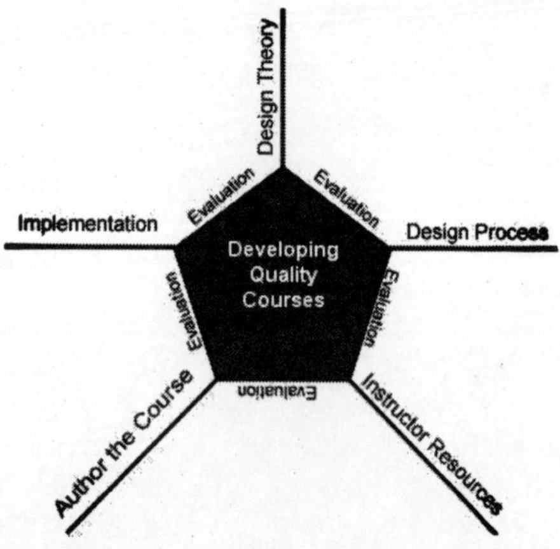

this world. Words full of laughter, words infused in pity, words that thrill, words that hurt-packed into them is the beauty of human life. We all have experienced various instructors in our life but we talk about very few of our instructors and most of the time we do crib about our instructors who once were trying to be our role models.

Having good qualifications for becoming a instructor does land up an individual into a job, but the success of the individual depends upon the way the individual is able to deliver the expected knowledge amongst the learners. We must realize the fact that a good instructor is born, not made and it is cruel on our part to expect each instructor to be the best instructor. For understanding instructors it would worthwhile for us to see through examples the differences amongst faculty members and how few fail to perform in the real life work environment.

Example 1: Faculty, *Abhijeet Chandra,* Abhijeet is well educated, expert in finance with a doctorate degree from central university of India. He is working in one leading business school based in North India, Abhijeet is very dedicated and dynamic and he is liked by the students as well as superiors. His students want him to stay in the institute and his superiors have lots of expectations from him. Abhijeet wants success and he wants to be seen as a successful individual in the society, hence is not satisfied with the salary being offered to him. In real life situation, the salary offered to Abhijeet is way below the acceptable standard of the academic industry. Abhijeet discussed his situation with his superior the advisor to the Chairman of his institute, and was told that his salary would be increased keeping in mind his level of commitment and sincerity. But the Chairman decided not to increase Abhijeet's salary and this made Abhijeet quit from his job. Though Abhijeet is a good instructor, he had great command over his subject and was considered as one of the best instructor, but he failed to survive in the work atmosphere and became victim of official politics.

Though Abhijeet possessed all qualities of a good instructor, but he wasn't able to satisfy the work culture of the education environment.

Example 2: *Dinesh Sharma,* Dinesh is working in one of the north India based business school and he is admired by his students as well the faculty members of the institute. Dinesh had vast experience of teaching in a school environment and then he applied for the post of lecturer in the business school and his candidature got accepted. Dinesh groomed himself well and satisfied all the segments of the business school from top management till the student community. His work was appreciated by all, but somehow few members of the top management changed, including the advisor to the Chairman and Director of the Institute and with the change of guard, situation of Dinesh changed in the organization.

His immediate boss dislikes his style of working and wants him to quit his job and for the same, his boss created a non-worthy working environment which made it difficult for Dinesh to survive in the organization, but as Dinesh is amongst one of the best faculty members of business school he had few members in the top management on his side he survived in the organization and continued to be one of the best faculty member.

Though these two examples are not enough for understanding the situations which force good faculty members to leave teaching and move on towards other career paths. We need to accept the reality that faculty members are also human beings and they have to go through tough times and the environment in which they work takes its toll on the faculty members.

Researcher like Miller said, "Learning to teach successfully is like learning to drive a car, learning to play bridge or golf or learning any other complicated performance is that the learner must develop still in several different operations all at once".

As we academicians the self-professed instructor trainers know, teaching techniques are often part of aids used for making the learners interested in the lessons, explaining the content and remembering it by heart during teaching. In order to achieve the teaching objective, the instructor must seek help of a teaching technique to mark the knowledge in the brains of the learners. Teaching techniques are used to make the lesson interesting, effective and a success and it is always advised to the instructor that before entering the class, the instructor must have more than one plan of action during the day. Instructor should be well read and prepared before hand and must always be aware of the situations under which he or she may be asked to perform in present of the learners.

GENERAL TECHNIQUES OF TEACHING

General techniques of teaching are those in which the lesson is developed by creating interest in the learner. Each and every learner wants attention and the giving proper recognition as well as attention is in hands of individual instructor. We the academicians must give attention to the learning styles of the learners and think about providing proper feedback and instructor to the learners. Individuals learn and process information in different ways. Most learners deliver instruction in one way or other and we have often heard that one learner is smarter than other. Really this learner is just as different from the other, we hardly see any learner who would difficult for the instructor to handle. Training programs must take into account that all learners are different and organize learning process in a way that all learners benefit from the lesson.

PROCESS OF IDENTIFYING PERSON'S LEARNING STYLE

There are various ways to classify learning styles and most classifications are based on perceptual modalities in which our individual bodies absorb information and then use the information for future betterment. A learning style is a student's consistent way of responding to and using stimuli in the context of learning. Keefe (1979) defines learning styles as the "composite of characteristics cognitive, affective, and physiological factors that serve as relatively stable indicators of how a learner perceives, interacts with, and responds to the learning environment.

Learning styles are points along a scale that help us to discover the different forms of mental representations; however, they are not good characterizations of what people are or not like. We should not divide the population into a set of categories (i.e., visual and auditory learners). What these various instruments attempt to do is to allocate a person on some point on a continuum. In other words, do not pigeonhole people as we are all capable of learning under almost style, no matter what our preference is. The literature basically indicates that there is wide acceptance of the concept of learning styles, however, there is disagreement on how to measure learning style. Learning is associated with better understanding of the subject matter and once the instructor has gained understanding of the subject, he or she must enhance ability of using innovative instructional activities that relate to the diverse learning styles of learners.

Most researchers agree that we do have various learning styles and preferences, however, the research tends to agree that it is relative insignificant as it is far more important to match the presentation with the nature of the subject, such as providing correct learning methods, strategies, and context; than matching individual preferences (Coffield, 2004).

David Merrill (2000) has the best philosophy for using learning styles—instructional strategies should first be determined on the basis of the type of content to be taught or the goals of the instruction (the content-by-strategy interactions) and secondarily, learner styles and preferences are then used to adjust or fine-tune these fundamental learning strategies. Finally, content-by-strategy interactions take precedence over learning-style-by-strategy interactions regardless of the instructional style or philosophy of the instructional situation.

Most classifications of learning styles are based on perceptual modalities—the primary way our bodies take in information. Usually researchers classify learners into four classes:

- Visual,
- Auditory,
- Kinaesthetic
- Tactile

CONNECTING FAMILIES AND EDUCATORS

The old saying "It Takes a Village to Raise a Child" comes to mind when considering the public education of children with Learning Differences, which are commonly referred to as Learning Disabilities. To be clear from the start, within our current systems of education, these Learning Differences are disabilities but do not have to remain as disabilities. The fostering of a co-operative relationship between those who are involved in public education could ameliorate barriers that create the condition of disability for those whose function exists outside of the current definition of 'norm'.

To turn a Learning Disability into a Learning Difference, it is imperative that Ministries, district school boards, local schools and families have a symbiotic relationship that remains focused on delivering the optimal education for all children. For a child with a Learning Difference an optimal education requires some additional, but not arduous, supports.

A disability is created when impairment is attempting to negotiate an environment that is fixed and rigid in its structure. The inflexibility of the environment then creates a barrier that the impairment is unable to pass. This barrier has disabled the impairment. If we were to make the environment flexible in a way that negates the barrier found within the environment, then the impairment is able to move past the barrier rendering the impairment no longer disabled. I would suggest that it is arguable to state that children with Learning Differences are disabled; but instead, we might consider that their educational environments are disabling. Disability therefore is not located within the child; it is located within the environment.

Unfortunately, the experience of parents, whose children have Learning Differences within the educational system, is wrought with conflicting messages and inconsistent supports. One parent may feel that their child's situation is supported and under control, while another may experience open hostility, blame and excuses. The cause of the variability in experiences can be found within the environment. Your experience of Special Education will depend on the perspective of those who participate in your child's education. Because those who are involved with the education of your child may change on a yearly basis, the experience of Special Education may also change, due much to the fact that not all educators or education administrators have a knowledge base in special education. One condition that seems to persist for the families of children with Learning Differences is the condition of marginalization and isolation.

Special Education is structured on many levels with policies and directives intended for the consistent delivery of educational supports to every child. Policies are concepts that define what is available and what you can expect from Special Education. It is important for parents to understand these policies and directives because once a child has been labelled with a Learning Disability your experience becomes one of being 'politicized'. In other words, you and your child's experiences are dependent on these public policies and their implementation. Knowledge of Special Education policy is a very powerful advocacy tool for a parent to ensure their children's needs are being met within the day-to-day processes of education.

The top tier of policy formation in education is the Provincial Ministry. These policies are the most important policies for parents to understand as they transcend both the district school board and local school's policies. All other policy developed pertaining to Special Education must be (although sometimes is not) designed to meet and reflect the Ministry's policy. The Ministry also provides funding to school boards specifically to support the delivery of special education programs and services.

The Ministry of Ontario has been moving in a direction that fosters the building of relationships that facilitate improved support for students within the classroom. The ministry acknowledges that the relationship between schools and families has historically been in need of improvement by turning their focus onto this issue. On December 1, 2005 the Minister of Education announced a new provincial policy to support parents' involvement in their children's education (People for Education, 2006). It has been recognized that parents need to be partners in the education of their children. It is of particular importance that parents of children with Learning Differences be full partners in the education of their children, if we are to achieve the level of support required for their optimal educational experience.

As previously stated the Ministry of Education creates the overreaching policies of special education and provides the funding for these services and supports to the local district school boards. At this second tier of administration, programs and their delivery are designed for the services your child receives at their local schools. The district school boards have a difficult task, which relies on a good relationship with both the Ministry and the families they service, to be successful.

District school boards have autonomy in their program development, creating both positive and negative aspects for Special Education. On a positive note a district school board has a better understanding of the needs in their specific area and are able to tailor their programs to the specific needs presented within that area. The negative aspect of this autonomy is that many of the conceptual underpinnings of Ministry's policies can be lost in translation or creatively usurped for what a board may feel is a more pressing need (these are usually of an economic nature). Ultimately the success or failures of programs are dependent on the perspective of those who design the programs, in relation to disability. If a program is designed with disability located within the child, the result will be entirely different than if disability is located within the environment. The focus of disability being within the child will result in the need of the child to adapt; verses if disability is located within the environment, then the environment is in need of adapting.

Finally, once Special Education policies have been filtered through the district school boards, the local schools carry out the programs and services as stipulated by their board. This is where most parents will form relationships that "appear" to directly affect their children. The experience and relationships for families at this level depend largely on the administrator of the school, the principal. The principal sets the tone for their staff in relation to Special Education and Learning Differences and acts as an ambassador of the district school board. The Principal is placed between you and the district school board. His or her job is either helped or

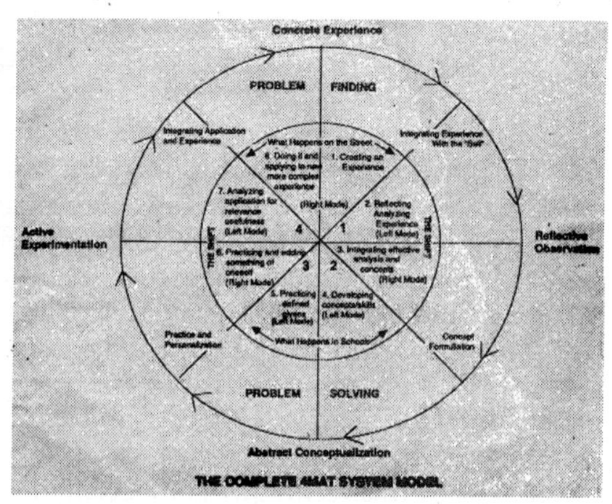

THE COMPLETE 4MAT SYSTEM MODEL

hindered in regards to special education, depending on how the district school board chooses to address the programs designed to meet the Ministry's mandated policies. At this level the interconnected relationships of all levels of education are reflected in the implementation of service to your child.

It is obvious that your relationship with the principal of your child's school is a very important one to nurture, but is not the only relationship that directly affects the educational experience of children with Learning Differences. It takes a village to raise and educate a child and although many view the Ministry, the district school boards, the local schools and their families as separate entities, they are not. These public institutions are all a part of the village that is helping us to raise our children.

As in any village, the relationships we foster with our community members shape and define our well-being and sense of belonging. Our village consists of many people with different abilities, impairments and perspectives as part of the 'normal' human condition. Our relationships can influence perspectives that create our environment. Our environments can determine whether we are fully co-operating members of our village. As parents it is up to us to foster relationships that turn the perspective of our village away from creating an environment that is disabling to our children with Learning Differences; but instead, focuses on the removal of the environmental aspects of education that create disability for learning.

EXPLANATION TECHNIQUE

Explanation is the technique in which every idea regarding the content is made clear or at least the instructor tries to make each and every idea clear. It is the technique in which an extremely difficult concept is explained in a simplified manner. Every problem, confusion and difficulty of the lesson are analyzed and explained by way of explanation in such a simple language that every learner of the class may pick up the core of the concept very easily. Instructors who want learners to explore all the ideas and develop deep understanding of the subject matter with a long lasting vision use explanation technique very often. Use of this technique is especially needed in teaching the difficult words, sentences and explaining them on the basis of previous knowledge.

It is especially needed in teaching the difficult words, sentences and explaining them on the basis of previous knowledge. For example, when a instructor tells the meaning of some difficult words, he tries to make its meaning clear by its origin, opposite word, use in sentences, etc. During language teaching, explanation technique is used in the following forms:

- Acting—Explaining the difficult words by acting.
- Using in a Sentence—Using difficult words in sentences.
- Stating Synonyms—Explaining difficult words by such simple words, which carry the same meaning.
- Stating Opposite Words—Difficult words are interpreted by telling opposite words of the difficult words.
- Analysis—Difficult words are explained by analyzing.
- Telling Origin—To clarify the words by telling their origin.

LIMITATIONS OF EXPLANATION TECHNIQUE

For using this technique the instructor should have some expected efficiency which the instructor might be lacking. It is difficult to determine the limit to which explaining should be used and the basis of explanation is concluded. Explanation technique might fail to draw a whole picture of the contents before the learners. The instructor must keep in mind the following factors before using the explanation technique:

- Explanations should be according to the understanding level of the learner.
- Explanation should be done when the learners are absorbed in the learning process and they are engrossed in the learning process.
- Explanation should not occur without any need, this wastes the time and energy.
- Explanation should occur only for those points which a student might be able to understand with minimum

efforts, it is great mistake to explain meaningless concepts and ideas.

- The instructor should have deep knowledge of the subject and in its absence; the explanation would be erroneous and irrelevant. Explanation should not be stretched and if by mistake any over-confident instructor does that he or she will make the learners lose interest in the lesson and the learners might feel bored.
- Explanation should be simple, correct and in clear words. Use of difficult complicated words makes the teaching and learning process a failure. Hence, the instructor should have mastery of the language.
- Explanation should be limited and relevant so that the interest of the learners may be maintained.
- Explanation should not be in the form of advice, because learners don't like such advice.
- Instructor should carry on maximum explanation in higher level and minimum in lower level.
- When explanation is over, the instructor must ask questions from the learners. He should repeat whatever the learners fail to understand.

> THE HINDU
>
> Online edition of India's National Newspaper
> Tuesday, Sep. 03, 2002
>
> **Making of a Good Instructor**
>
> Teaching needs three qualities. Knowledge is the first. The ability to pass it on to others, what we usually call communication skill, is the next. Aptitude is the third. Which quality of an instructor is tested in the so-called eligibility tests?
>
> INSTRUCTORS ARE born and not made. An instructor is a social entity. A poor instructor tells. A good instructor teaches. An excellent instructor demonstrates. An outstanding instructor motivates. Time and again we hear these proverbial sayings from various sources at different

occasions, especially as we near a instructor's day. If any of the above is correct, how can one find an instructor through a test, whether it is conducted by the UGC (National eligibility test) or by the States (state eligibility test)?

In a democratic country like India, any one with a medical degree from a recognised institution and medical council's registration can practise as a doctor. One can practise as a lawyer, if he has degree in law and completes the formalities of bar council. Engineers can get a job right away from the college campus through campus placement cells. But to become an instructor a person has to write a minimum of three examinations. A post-graduate degree examination followed by one for a degree in teaching and then the so-called eligibility tests. Even this does not get one a job, but only qualifies one for it!

Teaching needs three qualities. Knowledge is the first. The ability to pass it on to others, what we usually call communication skill, is the next. Aptitude is the third. Which quality of an instructor is tested in the so-called eligibility tests? Is it the first one? That is unbelievable. Any recognized educational institution in India offers a post-graduate degree after completion of a minimum of semester course. The incumbent is then examined at the end of each semester by a qualified and experienced faculty appointed directly by the supreme body of the university called the syndicate. One has to prove the ability before these examiners. A post-graduate paper is valued independently by two experts. If necessary, there will be a third evaluation as well. In science subjects, the performance in the practical examinations has to be satisfactory. There will be a project evaluation. And then, there is the viva-voce test. One has to go through all these complex and difficult manoeuvres before getting the degree. Then, which knowledge not proved in the above is tested in the eligibility test in just around three hours, even if it is a UGC standard test or eligibility tests run by the states?

We must also recall that these tests, in at least some states, are reduced to the level of an ordinary entrance examination for engineering and medicine. There is a group of expert educationalists who believe that an objective model entrance test is inadequate even for engineering and medicine. They recommend IIT model entrance tests. Then, how can we justify the objective model instructor eligibility tests now in force in some states?

The second quality, that is, communication skill, cannot be found through a test either. It would be like studying acting through post. Either you have it or you do not. It is as simple as that. One can never create this. You can only discover whether you have it or not. But if it is within you, it grows with experience. So to have this you have to become a instructor. But to become a instructor you need this. Looks like a vicious circle, isn't it?

Which component of the teaching is more important? Is it the knowledge or the ability to pass it on? Well, it very much depends on the class one is teaching. If you are in a post-graduate class, knowledge is more important than presentation. The students of the class are filtered stuff. They expect information from the instructor. Half the knowledge is where to find it. If this is true, they need only know where to find things much more than the thing itself. But if one is teaching in a school or plus two class, the ability to communicate is more important than the knowledge itself. Here 'teaching is innovation' become true.

We have to find independent, natural and new methods for presentation of the subject and the topics. The emphasis has to be more on how to tell than what to tell. The classes have to be interactive. Teaching has to be a dialogue and not a monologue. This would mean we should have patience towards questions, no matter how silly they are. Those who are successful in these respects alone can become good instructors at this stage. Even with a limited knowledge a person can become a good instructor, if he/she has these abilities. Here you study to teach and then teach to study more.

The aptitude for teaching too cannot be found through a test. It can be decided only by the persons themselves. Here again, it comes to your mind that you want to become a instructor, or you would never. Only those motivated to this profession opt for it. Others withdraw from the race. The motivation sets in early. Sitting in a good instructor's class, those with aptitude always probe whether they can teach like this and then believe they can. Similarly, sitting in a poor instructor's class, the experience might dissuade even those with possible aptitude to opt out of the profession. Thus our aptitude is well influenced by the classes we sit in and the instructors who teach us in our student days from primary school to college.

So these tests cannot really test knowledge. They cannot test communication skills or aptitude either. The tests are reduced to the level of a mere common test for various people who come from different streams and who have obtained degrees from different institutions. But if we have a method to measure marks obtained from different recognised institutions by the same yardstick, these tests become superfluous.

The Birla Institute of Technology, commonly known as BITS Pilani, is one of the country's leading educational institutions. There is no entrance test for admission to courses here. They have got a method to standardise marks from different institutions. We should adopt something like this to dispense with eligibility tests. These tests never determine any eligibility. If ever they do test anything, it is only the luck and time of the person.

Didn't we have famous devoted instructors before entrance and eligibility tests were even thought of? They live in our minds for ever. What eligibility test did they write? This leads us to a simple straightforward truth. No matter who conducts the tests be it the state or the UGC and no matter how transparent and credible it is, the ability of a instructor is decided in class rooms and that too by students and not by entrance and eligibility tests.

V. MAHADEVA IYER

EXPOSITION TECHNIQUE

This technique means the presentation of facts of a lesson in a definite, logical manner and clear, understandable and simplified way that all the learners may learn the most difficult things very easily. It is used in the teaching of all the subjects but it is more beneficial in language teaching.

Following precautions should be taken care of while using the explosion technique:

- The subject to be expositioned should be according to the interest and the mental level of the learners. In other words, the exposition should be appropriate.
- The instructor should use simple, clear and interesting language.
- Difficult parts, facts and various aspects of the lesson should be carefully elucidated.
- The correct exposition of any subject is possible only when the instructor is familiar with all parts of the subject. Hence, the subject should be presented properly, before the learners.

Limitations

Instructors must accept the reality that it is difficult to decide about the appropriateness of the exposition because it is difficult to explore which aspect of the subject is to be exposed. It is not an easy job to determine the specific aspects of the lesson while exposing it because no criterion can be decided easily. Exposition can only succeed when the instructor arranges the facts in a logical sequence in advance and this not every instructor's job. It is visible that due to differences amongst the learner community, every learner has difference in receptivity when it comes to learning of any complicated issue. Keeping all the differences in mind, the instructor should be prepared with any unexpected event as no definite opinion can be formed regarding the adequacy of the exposition.

Principles of Use

(1) The instructor should present the lesson before the learners after determining the objectives of the lesson.
(2) In order to make the exposition effective, the entire lesson should be divided into clear and natural units. The first unit should be made clear to the learners and then next. Each unit should accommodate as much ideas which a pupil can acquire conveniently.
(3) A simple, clear and effective language should be used.
(4) Exposition should be clear and definite.
(5) The instructor should have sufficient knowledge about the attitudes of the learners.
(6) He should eliminate the errors committed by himself. He should think over the subject-material and he must remove the doubts of the learners.
(7) Only those main things should be stressed specifically which are directly related to the lesson. It can be written on black board for clarification if it is considered necessary.
(8) Interesting and understandable, examples, illustrations, pictures and devices should be used frequently.
(9) The speed of exposition should be according to their intelligence and their power of understanding. A fast-talk by the instructor obstructs the understanding of the learners.
(10) The instructor should use all the techniques like narration, description, explanation, etc. and as the need arises, he should allow the learners to ask the questions. Not only this, when the exposition is over, the instructor will have to inquire by questioning the limit upto which the explanation succeeded.

STORY-TELLING TECHNIQUE

Story-telling means to recite or to tell a story. The complicated and minute details of a subject are made so easy through story telling that all the learners understand it very easily. Psychologically, young learners do not have mental development enough to acquire minute and complex ideas easily. But, as they show natural interest in listening a story, they grasp the knowledge presented in the form of a story. Through a story, the imaginative and reasoning powers of the learners are developed in such a way, that their moral and social qualities are developed. They assimilate the knowledge of any subject very easily. They acquire knowledge in the form of a story with great interest. The story telling technique is generally used in' the lower Classes. But it can be used successfully in the higher classes as well. In the lower classes it is used for the teaching of science, language and social subjects, but in higher classes it 'can be used for teaching subjects like history, civics, economics and commerce, etc. Story-telling is an art. Some people are expert in this art by birth, but these skills can be acquired and expertise can be achieved by learning those skills.

Principle of Story-telling

(1) The story-teller should prepare a complete mental-picture of the various elements of the story. Then its theme and ideas should be presented in a logical manner.
(2) Before telling a story, the important elements of the knowledge should be understood by learning them. The crammed words make the story dull.
(3) The characters of the story should be according to the characters of the close surroundings of the learners.
(4) The story-telling should occur when the learners are interested in it.
(5) The class-environment should be peaceful. In a noisy environment, telling a story is mere wastage of time.
(6) While telling a story, the mental stage, interests and emotional characteristics of the learners should not be over-looked.
(7) The language of the story should be easy, correct and clear.
(8) The story-teller should have fluctuations in his voice.
(9) The style of the story-telling should be natural, emotional and attractive. It should not have any sort of artificiality.

(10) There should be a direct relationship of the story with the subject.

(11) The story-teller should develop the imagination, curiosity and motivation of the learners more and more by using his own imaginative power.

(12) The story should be used as a means, not as a goal.

SUPERVISED STUDY TECHNIQUE

Supervised study technique is based on the principles of individual differences and activity. Its birth took place in the form of a reaction to the traditional techniques. Keeping in view the individual differences, every pupil is provided with an opportunity to do his respective task and study, and the instructor solves his individual problems by supervising his tasks as a friend, helper and a guide. Hence, both pupil and the instructor are active. Though it is not possible to supervise every task of the learners, but important tasks can be supervised. After instructing the learners regarding certain particular tasks, their activities can be supervised. This technique is used for all the learners of the class especially backward learners.

Types

1. *Conference Plan*. Conferences are organized time to time, whole the problems of the learners are sorted out by mutual consultations.
2. *Special Instructor Plan*. In this plan, specialized instructors remove the difficulties, errors and misconceptions of the learners.
3. *Divided Period Plan*. In this plan, two instructors supervise the tasks of the learners in the duration.
4. *Double Period Plan*. In this plan, two periods are provided to the learners to study the same subject-matter. In the first period, learners are instructed to study after presenting the background of the decided subject. In the second period, learners study that subject and the instructor supervises their activities. Mabel E. Simpson has divided two collective periods of minutes by using this plan as follows:

Review	25 Minutes
Assignment	25 Minutes
Physical Exercise	35 Minutes
Study of the assignments	35 Minutes
Total	120 Minutes

5. *Periodical Plan*. In this plan, learners are instructed to do predetermined tasks. After some definite period, their progress is supervised. Hence, the instructor performs the function of supervision and guidance weekly, fortnightly or monthly.

Precautions

(1) To make this technique a success, an instructor must possess insight and resourcefulness.
(2) While using this technique, the instructor should plan in such a way so that a scientific attitude may be developed.
(3) A habit of working in a friendly way should be created by this supervised study technique.
(4) Self-confidence and self-dependence should be developed by using this technique.
(5) The tasks assigned to the learners should be according to their mental and physical abilities and interests.

TEACHER EDUCATION IN CHINA

Pre-service Training of Primary and Secondary School Teachers

General Higher Teacher Education

General higher teacher education in China aims mainly at the training of secondary school teachers. In 1998, there were 229 general higher education institutions in China with an enrolment of 690,000. Normal universities, teacher-training institutes and teacher training colleges enrol graduates from senior secondary schools. Four-year programs are offered for training senior secondary school teachers, 2-year or 3-year programs are mainly to train teachers for junior secondary schools. The specialties are as follows Pedagogy, Pre-school Education, Special Education, Psychology, Educational Technology, Chinese Language and Literature, Languages and Literature of Minority Nationalities, Ideological and Political Education, History, English, Russian, Japanese, Mathematics and applied Mathematics, Computer Science, Physics, Chemistry, Biology, Geography, Music, Fine Arts and Physical Education. Besides, postgraduate programs are offered in general higher teacher education institutions. At the same time, general higher teacher education institutions are playing active parts in providing in-service training for secondary school teachers.

Regular Secondary Teacher Education

Regular secondary teacher education aims mainly at training teachers for primary schools, kindergartens and special education. In 1998, there were 875 regular secondary colleges of teacher training in China with 920,000 enrolments. Out of these 875 colleges, there were 811 regular secondary teacher training schools, 61 for pre-school education and 3 for special education.

The main task for regular secondary teacher education is to prepare teachers for primary school education. They enrol graduates from junior secondary schools, and offer either 3-year programs or 4-year programs. The courses are made up of 4 parts £° compulsory courses, optional courses, teaching practice and extracurricular activities. Compulsory courses are £° Ideological and Political Education, Chinese £¨ including Methodology of Chinese Teaching in Primary Schools £©, Mathematics £¨ including Methodology of Mathematics Teaching in Primary Schools £©, Physics, Chemistry, Biology, History, Geography, Psychology, Pedagogy for Primary School, Basic Audio-visual Education, Physical Education, Music, Fine Arts, Laboring Skills, and Basics of Computer Application. In accordance with the regional education needs, the optional courses include subjects that help broadening and deepening the students' knowledge and fostering their interests and aptitudes. Furthermore, vocational and technical subjects are offered to meet the requirements of the local economic development. Teaching practice includes visits to primary schools, educational survey, teaching probation and experimental teaching. The extracurricular activities are conducted by means of lectures, organizing special interest groups and conducting social surveys to educate students in disciplines, science and technology, arts and sports.

—*The main task of secondary pre-school teacher training schools is to educate kindergarten teachers.* In 1998, there were 61 secondary pre-school teacher training schools in China with 58,000 enrollments £® In addition, such programs are offered in some regular secondary teacher training colleges and vocational senior secondary schools. Secondary pre-school teacher training schools enrol graduates from junior secondary schools, offering 3-year or 4-year programs. The curriculums consist of 4 parts £° compulsory courses, optional courses, teaching practice and extracurricular activities. Compulsory courses include £° Ideological and Political Education, Chinese, Mathematics, Chemistry, Physics, Biology, Geography, History, Basic Audio-visual Education, Health Protection for Kindergarten Children, pre-school Psychology, Survey of Pre-school Education, Design and Instructions of Pre-school Educational Activities, Music, Fine Arts, Dancing, Physical Education and Laboring Skills. Geared to the requirements of local kindergartens, optional courses are designed to broaden the students, knowledge and develop their interests and special skills. Teaching practice includes visits to local kindergartens, on-the-spot observation of kindergarten children's mental and physical growth, teaching probation and student teaching themselves, and services for kindergartens. Extracurricular activities are intended to promote teaching in science and technology as well as in arts and sports through lectures, get-togethers and social surveys.

—*The main task of secondary special teacher-training schools is to educate special education teachers for primary schools.* In 1998, there were 33 secondary special education teacher-training institutions in China, 3 out of which were fully devoted to special education institutions.

Secondary teacher training institutes for special education offer three specialties£° education for the deaf, for the blind and for the mentally retarded £® Normally, they enrol graduates from junior secondary schools and the schooling lasts either 4 years or 3 years. The courses are made up of 4 parts that are compulsory courses, optional courses, teaching practice and extracurricular activities. The compulsory courses are classified into two categories £° public and specialized compulsory courses. The public ones include Ideological and Political Education, Chinese, Mathematics, Physics, Chemistry, Biology, History, Geography, Music, Physical Education, Fine Arts, Basic Pedagogy, Basic Psychology, Introduction to Special Education and Laboring Skills £® The specialized ones are separately offered for the above-mentioned three specialties. They include Psychology, Pedagogy, Methodology and other courses for prevention and examination of deformity. Altogether there are 22 specialized compulsory courses. The optional courses are based on the local needs for special primary education, including subjects that are helpful to broaden and deepen students' knowledge, to develop their interests and special skills, and vocational and technical subjects to meet the demands of local special education. Teaching practice includes visiting, probating and assisting special education teachers to organize activities, educational surveys and student teaching themselves. Extracurricular activities provide education in science and technology, arts and sports through lectures, get-togethers and social surveys, and through organizing students to coach voluntarily in special schools and local educational organizations.

In addition, optional courses of special education are offered in regular secondary schools of teacher training so as to enable their graduates to meet the future challenges of having handicapped children to study in the mainstream.

Teacher Education for Ethnic Minorities

China is a unified multi-ethnic nation with 56 ethnic

minority groups £® The population of these minorities is 108 million accounting for 8.98 £¥ of the total. Education of minority ethnic groups constitutes an important part in the national education undertaking. The country encourages the expansion of teacher education for minorities to promote the development of education in the regions where minority peoples reside. A group of higher teacher training institutions and colleges and secondary teacher training schools are responsible for teaching and training minority teachers. Teacher Training Center in the North-west and English Teacher Training Center in the South-west are established in the regions where the minority people concentrate. Parts of the nation's institutions and comprehensive universities also offer programs for training minority education teachers. The reform of minority teacher education is undergoing continuously and it is on the way to train versatile teachers with practical skills.

—China Education and Research Network

6

Cultural Awareness in the Classroom

Since last few years, I have been trying to understand the meaning of culture and have been searching if the culture lies somewhere deep which could be learnt only by experiencing culture. Different researchers and anthropologists have given different answers to the question, "*What is culture?*" Each school of thought has a different perspective on culture. To my mind, all the thoughts make sense, but the moment I try to compare them up against one another, I find them contradictory and confusing. Culture might include traditions, customs, assumptions, expectations and common points of reference. Currency isn't a conceptual aspect of culture.

We regularly speak and hear the word 'culture' around—but what exactly do we mean? Take a look at the list here and select the concepts we should consider when we look into a culture other than our own.

- Customs
- Traditions
- Assumptions

- Currency
- Expectations
- Common points of references

COMPONENTS OF CULTURE

The foreign language teaching profession in the United States published a comprehensive set of standards for foreign language education, including standards for culture (National Standards in Foreign Language Education Project, 1996). They based their definition of culture on three connected dimensions, products, practices, perspectives. Somehow seen in broad terms, culture consists of artifacts, actions, and meanings.

When we teach a class of learners brought up in a different culture from ours, we have two main aims:

- To teach them the English language.
- To teach them modern methods of learning.
- To make them aware of the differences between the culture of the English-speaking countries and the culture of their native country.
- To understand the need of the learners and modify the learning process as per the level of learners in new culture.

However, during the process of this, we may have to deal with a variety of false assumptions that are easily made, and less easily overcome. False assumptions make it difficult for a new instructor as well as learner to develop mutual respect and confidence and this very aspect hinders academic and personal development. Instructor development is must for the betterment of learners and for development professionally, instructor must be prepared to learn, unlearn and relearn. Recently at an HR Summit held at Guru Gobind Singh Indraprastha University, Delhi, *Professor Prev Vrat, former Vice-Chancellor* of *UP Technical University* said, "India is not a poor country, it is a poorly managed country". According to Professor Vrat, Indian as well as Asian Education needs overhauling and the teachers must be role models, teachers must have the will and vigor to support and fulfil the need and demand of the learner community. India being a multi-state and multi-cultural society provides a goody bag of mixed cultures and beliefs which in itself if managed properly can do wonders for the society and world at large.

MISINTERPRETATION

We humans act differently in a different environment and our personality traits play an important role in the grooming of an individual. It is relatively easy for an instructor and a class to misunderstand each other and make false assumptions. For example, in many non-English-speaking cultures, learners are brought up with more passive behaviors when interacting with adults.

ASKING FOR HELP

A learner may be less willing to ask an instructor for extra help or to admit that they don't understand. This can lead to assumptions that non-English-speaking learners are less intelligent than their native English-speaking peers.

PERCEIVED AGGRESSION

At the same time, non-English-speaking learners can quickly absorb cultural biases against English-speakers who come from a more driven and ambitious educational community than they may be accustomed to. The teacher's attitude may be perceived as aggressive by some learners, who will then be even less willing to participate or ask questions.

OVERCOMING BIAS

We should try to overcome preconceived notions about different cultures and also help our learners to overcome biases against our culture. In that way we will create a learning environment where everyone is valued for their unique heritage. This is easy said but difficult to do in real world, the instructor as well as learners all fall prey to biases and staying away from this situation comes by living and working in different work environments.

CULTURAL THEORY

We all need to understand the role of culture in relation to classroom environment if we intend to work in a multi-cultural society. There are many academic studies and intellectuals are involved in research on international culture, we are going to look at the work of Geert Hofstede. Hofstede's ideas were initially based on a large research project into national cultural differences across a multinational corporation, and later expanded to cover students and other professions and to cover more than 70 countries. From the initial results and later additions, Hofstede developed a model that identifies five 'dimensions of culture'.

HOFSTEDE'S FIVE DIMENSIONS OF CULTURE

Power Distance

In the English as a Foreign Language classroom the teacher is likely to be seen as a powerful person. In those countries where there is a large 'power distance', it is natural for students to be deferential towards the teacher and may feel uncomfortable laughing or joking around with them. Teachers should be careful not to confuse unfriendliness with respect. Students from cultures where there is power distance in large may not participate much. They may find discussions and negotiations on what to do in the classroom quite strange as they are unused to decision-making. Your students will recognize that their teacher comes from another culture and make allowances when you laugh and joke with them but you need to be aware that their normal expectation of teacher is someone they respect, defer to and obey. Power distances scores are high for Latin, Asian and African countries and smaller for Germanic countries.

Individualism

As experienced teachers know, in every EFL classroom there is always one person who will always volunteer answers, will always come up with something different, with new ideas and comments or points of view. This person is however unlikely to come from a culture where individualism is low. If you are teaching in a more collectively-oriented culture, you can be less reliant on the individual who will always answer your questions or volunteer a viewpoint. In more collective cultures it is not normal to deliberately be different or to try to stand out from the crowd. This can be very frustrating if you ask students for an opinion or indeed disagree with other students. In some cultures students would be very unwilling to voice a different opinion, particularly if it is negative and even more so if it is critical of that student's country, in a public situation like a classroom. For example, if you are trying to get some noisy debates in your class in Jilin, China, for example, you may need to rethink your approach. Discussion classes will struggle to work. An alternative and more successful option would be to go for task-based problem-solving activities where students have to come up with a solution without having to express personal opinions.

Masculinity

So called 'masculine' cultures value competitiveness, assertiveness, ambition, and the accumulation of wealth and material possessions, whereas 'feminine' cultures place more value on relationships and quality of life. Masculinity is high in Japan, in some European countries like Germany, Austria and Switzerland and moderately high in Anglo countries. In contrast, Masculinity is low in Nordic countries and in the Netherlands and moderately in some Latin and Asian countries like France, Spain and Thailand.

Uncertainty Avoidance Index (UAI)

The Uncertainty Avoidance Index indicates to what extent a culture programs its members to feel comfortable in unknown or surprising, i.e. different from usual, situations. Uncertainty avoiding cultures try to minimize the possibility of such situations by strict laws and rules, safety and security measures, and on the philosophical and religious level by a belief in absolute Truth; 'there can only be on Truth and we have it.' People in uncertainty avoiding countries are also more emotional, and motivated by inner nervous energy. Uncertainty avoiders are going to like planned and structured activities and will seek rules for the language you teach them. They may also be more intolerant of the views and cultures different from theirs. Uncertainty Avoidance scores are higher in Latin countries, in Japan and in German speaking countries. They are lower in Anglo, Nordic, and Chinese culture countries.

Long-term Orientation (LTO)

In the classroom environment those with a stronger short-term orientation may seem 'serious'. They are in the class to learn English in order to fulfil their goals. In addition, they may have been educated in a traditional and formal way. They may need to be convinced that communicative activities such as simulations and role plays are not just games but are valid controlled and free practice tools. A long-term-orientation is mostly found in East Asian countries, in particular China, Japan and South Korea. The long term oriented students will be very concerned about losing 'face'. Expect them to be reticent about speaking out for fear of making a mistake. You may also find that they excel in writing but feel less comfortable about speaking.

Korean Students *vs.* UK Teacher

Here is an summary comparison example. It compares Korean and UK culture (using a student's/teacher example) across the five dimensions

Power Distance—The teacher is happy for students to treat him or her informally and to retreat the students as equals. Korean students expect the teacher to be formal and will seek to treat him or her with respect and deference, rather than as an equal.

Individualism—The teacher comes from highly individualistic culture where doing your own thing and finding yourself (for example by travelling to Korea to teach), is applauded. Entrepreneurs are highly valued and differences are celebrated. This is fairly alien to Korean students, they tend to seek the right way to do things rather than wishing to be different. As a rule they do not want to be different and do not admire those who are.

Masculinity—The UK teacher is from a culture that encourages competition. The Korean students prefer to collaborate and nurture.

Uncertainty Avoidance—The teacher is likely to enjoy new challenges and changes and the students prefer traditional ways.

Long-term Orientation—Again the teacher and the students are poles apart in their values.

Chinese Students vs. American Teacher

Now take a look at this example comparing Chinese students and an American teacher.

Power Distance—The American teacher is likely to prefer a relaxed informal classroom atmosphere. The students expect the teacher to be the leader and will treat him with respect rather than instant friendship.

Individualism—The American teacher is likely to be highly individualistic and to recognize the value of being different, of being a bit of a character with his or her own views and ideas. The Chinese student does not share this admiration of that which is different but instead seeks to work for the good of the group.

Masculinity—Here our American and Chinese are both likely to be warm and caring rather than competitive and driven.

Uncertainty Avoidance—Again our Chinese and Americans are reasonably similar.

Long-term Orientation—Here our two cultures are poles apart. For the Chinese, saving face is vital. For the Americans, having a go is more admirable.

Bear in mind that these cultural differences describe or tendencies and not characteristics of individuals in every country you can find individuals who do not share some typical values and beliefs of their culture. Usually those are in the ones who have some experience of interacting with other cultures.

Cultural Faux-PAS

If you as an instructor don't know enough about the

culture of the country you are teaching in, which of these faux pas are you likely to commit?

- Teach inappropriate grammar
- Use inappropriate body language
- Bring up topics that are taboo
- Dress in an inappropriate way
- Fail to greet a person or bid them farewell in the right way

All of these are potential faux pas, except teaching grammar as there is no cultural aspect to grammar.

Andrew's Experience

Every EFL/ESL teacher who have ever taught overseas has made a cultural faux-pas at some time. Here you can see some examples.

Take Andrew's experience for example, as he explains here:

> "I was teaching in Jakarta, and I found it very difficult to pronounce their names. Sometimes I just touched them individually on the arm or back either with my right or my left hand when I wanted them to speak. Imagine my horror when gradually week by week students stopped coming because of this!"

You need to think about what might be the reason for this. In reality it was discovered that in their country it was inappropriate for anyone to touch another person with their left hand.

Christine's Experience

Christine had a similar experience, as she explains here:

> "I was teaching irregular verbs to my students in Saudi Arabia during one lesson, and to help get the concepts across we were playing bingo with the verbs! To spice up the activity I asked all the students to put a very small sum of money into a kitty—but many of the students refused point blank!"

COMMON CULTURAL DIFFERENCES

Let's take a look at some important cultural differences to be aware of and potential cultural pitfalls you could fall foul of in your first teaching position.

Shaking Hands

There are different traditions of greeting people in different countries. For example, in Russia men usually shake hands when they see each other for the first time during the day (whereas women never shake hands). You may see your male students shake hands with each other; however, the teacher (male or female) is not expected to shake hands with students.

How are you?

If you ask a Russian 'How are you?' they may take the question too literally and launch into a lengthy account of their latest achievements or family problems. They are unlikely to ask 'How are you?' in return because it is not a traditional greeting in their culture. A good idea is to explain the English custom of asking 'How are you?' to your students from the start. Tell them what the usual responses to the question are.

A Chinese Greeting

When Chinese people meet each other, they often say, "Have you had your meal yet?" which more of a friendly greeting than of a question of concern, but foreigners, not familiar with such a form of greeting, tend to find it rather awkward. Another common form of address if you meet someone in the street is asking 'Where are you going?' instead of 'hello'. If your students ask you these questions you need to be aware that they are attempting to great you rather than being nosey or impolite.

Taboo Subjects

Getting together with your students to discuss a topic is a great way to encourage conversation skills, but be careful to choose a suitable subject. My own experience of China is different, I personally rate China is a wonderful country and the students are certainly one of the best in the world. The administration of the college where I taught in the orientation meeting itself made it clear to us that we should never talk about *Religion, Tibet, Taiwan, Tiananmen Square* with our students as these topics were unacceptable in the Chinese culture.

Unless you really know your students, you should avoid discussing any contentious subjects. The discussion about who should stay at home and look after housework is a non-starter in many countries, as is the discussion about the merits of cohabitating before marriage.

As an instructor you must think about *taboo subjects* and try to avoid them and you must think about the taboo subjects. What other global taboo subjects can you think of? Take some time and then try to reflect on a paper about the global taboos.

People from different cultures think differently and act in a way which might be acceptable one culture and not acceptable in another. Following issues will be seen as taboo:

- Discussions about Sex
- Discussions about Religion
- Discussions related to Politics
- Sex, drugs, and alcohol
- Any criticism of a country which appears in the international press, e.g. human rights issues in China
- Wars and political unrest
- Some aspects of history
- Homosexuality in some cultures
- Challenging cultural norms
- The value of honesty
- Attitudes toward children
- Attitudes toward animals

I have noticed that writing name of any individual in red ink is seen as a death sentence in China. If by chance someone teaches in China, then the instructor must avoid writing names of students in red ink.

Gestures and Body Language

Gestures and body language are thought to by some to convey more meaning than the actual words spoken. Naturally just as languages differ so do body languages. In many cultures certain things may be inappropriate or disrespectful. Some useful examples are:

- Touching the head, shoulders or back of an older person.
- The thumbs-up gesture is considered obscene in many countries.
- For a man to make any comment about a woman's appearance can be considered inappropriate.
- Point with one's index finger is considered impolite, especially when pointing at people.
- Politeness measured in terms of gallantry or etiquette is important e.g., standing up for a woman who approaches a table, giving a seat on the train/bus to an older person.

Giving Praise

Whereas giving praise can show natural warmth in some cultures, take a look at the following examples:

> A British professor once saw a Chinese wearing a pretty dress, she said to her, "You look very beautiful today". To her surprise, the student blushed and said timidly, "No, no. This is an ordinary dress".

On another occasion, she commented on a student's spoken English, "Your English is quite fluent". The student was quick to respond, "No, no. My English is quite poor". Their responses confused and piques the British professor, who might be thinking that the students rudely questioned her judgment. In reality, these students responded according to their cultural values.

In Arab countries, it is not a good idea to praise an object someone owns as they will feel obliged to give it to you as a present.

Appearance and Dress

Teachers should dress appropriately at all times. Depending where you are this will vary considerably. In most schools, in most parts of the world, teachers are expected to dress smartly. If you want to play it safe, avoid the scruffy jeans and vest top. Be careful about wearing modest clothing if you are teaching in a hot climate. Ask the school about the dress code beforehand you can take appropriate clothes from home. If you have visible body piercings do not be surprised if you are asked to remove them. In many countries it is considered inappropriate for a teacher to have any piercings. If you have green hair or Mohawk cut, do not be surprised if you don't get the job you are after. As a tip, if a prospective employer asks for a photo, do yourself a favour and send one of your more conservatives ones. If you don't look the part, you won't get the part!

Some other cultural differences should be gone through, we the instructors must take a look at the following other cultural differences:

- *Manners*: Sniffing, spitting, blowing your nose are acceptable in some cultures and very inappropriate in others.
- *Entering and leaving classroom* : Certain rituals may be involved and greetings are necessary in many cultures.
- "Yes"—"Yes" may mean, "I hear you" more than "I agree".
- *Length of pleasantries*: Length of pleasantries and greetings before getting down with business may vary.
- *Level of tolerance*: Level of tolerance for being around someone speaking a foreign (not understood) language may also vary

Task 1—Give your Friend Advice

If a friend of yours were going to foreign country to teach English, what advice would you give him or her to help them avoid cultural howlers in the classroom?

I advised one of my best friends from Canada. My friend was thinking about going abroad for teaching English but he wasn't too sure about South Korea and my advice for my friend was to think positive and move ahead to the foreign shore. I advised my friend to read details about South Korea, read about its history, its culture and scan newspapers as well as media for getting updates about South Korea. I also advised my friend to surf internet and go to chat rooms and interact with people who have been to South Korea earlier, so that he could get first hand information.

Some ideas which might be similar to yours are:

- Thoroughly research the culture of the country you will be teaching in.
- See if you can find out if there are any taboo subjects.
- Speak to other teachers about any mistakes they made.
- Ensure you understand the dress code and rules of the school you will be teaching in.
- If in doubt, play it safe!
- Build a good rapport with your class if they like their teacher they are more likely to forgive you any cultural faux-pas.

TEACHING A MONOCULTURAL CLASS

If you are going abroad then it is most likely that you be teaching a Monocultural class. The advantage of this is that you will be able to read up on the typical differences in culture as well as pronunciation and grammar problems that your students may have trouble with on account of their first language.

You will soon learn whether your students are likely to be active and collaborative or quieter and more passive. Whatever you do, do not try to change your class. You are a teacher of English language and it is not your job to educate your students on the merits of your culture or way of doing things, but it is likely that these will make great topics for discussions. If you can find out about the national dishes, holidays and customs of the country you are teaching in, you'll have some great material that every student knows something about. Many students enjoy teaching you about their culture.

Do bear in mind however that you may well have students in your class who are not nationals of the country you are teaching in or who have grown up in a different culture. This can require some delicate handling in some circumstances.

A MULTICULTURAL CLASS

The multicultural class is probably the preference of most teachers, given the choice. By multicultural we mean a mixture of nationalities. You are more likely to get this in your own country. The reality is more likely to be mixture of several main nationalities. The reality is more likely to be mixture of several main nationalities, across a number of cultures.

- *Equality—Do not tolerate bad behaviour* : The main issue for the EFL/ESL/EAP instructor with a multilingual class is to ensure that everyone gets on and respects each other. This starts with the instructor doing just that and never showing a preference for any particular nationality. Each nationality will have its own pronunciation problems and in some cases, students will find it hard to understand each other. Do not tolerate any form of ridicule for other students when a student makes a mistake. As an instructor you should not let your students make racist comments or at least signal your disapproval and move on.
- *Diversity—Make the most of diversity*: On other occasion get your students to enjoy their diversity. Savvy teachers can arrange group projects designed to encourage students to enter one share and explore one another's cultures. As a task-based discussion, get the class, in small groups, to imagine that they are going to open a 'fusion' restaurant featuring starters, main courses and desserts from all the countries represented in the group. Your class will be describing national dishes and will leave the lesson with a good appetite for supper!

- *Personality—Give power to quieter students*: If you have a class comprised of, for example, outgoing Brazilians and Italians and a few quieter Chinese and Japanese, you need to bear this in mind when you allocate your students to groups. While the quieter students may be happy to listen, the more outgoing ones can become resentful as they feel they are doing all the work. So, occasionally it is good to put the quieter ones into a group together and give them a chance to have their say.

BILINGUAL AND BICULTURAL

While your ultimate goal of teaching as second or foreign language is to create bilingual students, an additional goal should be to create students. Well trained instructor should practice cultural sensitivity and encourage students to learn about new cultures.

As Students learn to compare their old culture with their new culture, they can gain an appreciation of both without minimizing or denigrating either culture. Take a look at these activities that can help with this process.

Films: Watching and discussing films which have become an important part of your culture and which illustrate some typical features of your culture.

Polls: Taking polls of students' assumptions and beliefs about English culture and discussing the results.

Q&A: Encouraging question and answer sessions about the new culture while comparing it to students' native cultures, such as discussing popular television shows, slang, or other lifestyle characteristics.

Guest Speakers: Inviting guest speakers who have successfully integrated into the new culture but who are still active. This will demonstrate how biculturalism can enrich your life.

Task 2—Which of the following statements are examples of managing cultural issues incorrectly?

1. We should make our students accept the norms of our own country instead of the norms of their culture.

2. If we make a culture mistake, we will antagonize the class and lose students' respect.
3. If we make a cultural mistake it's best not to tell our colleagues about it as it may damage our reputation.
4. We must know almost everything about the culture of the country we are teaching in

Task 3—We should make our students accept the norms of our own country instead of the norms of their culture. We shouldn't make our students change their cultural norms and beliefs. English culture should not replace their culture. If we make a cultural mistake, we will antagonize the class and loose students' respect and if our students like us and trust us, an apology will suffice, and the mistake will soon be forgotten. If we make a cultural mistake it's best not to tell our colleagues about it as it may damage our reputation. It will not damage your reputation; your colleagues may help you avoid other blunders in the future, and you will give the less experienced teachers a chance to learn from your experience.

Circles of My Multicultural Self:
This activity requires 20-30 minutes.

Purpose: The Circles activity engages participants in a process of identifying what they consider to be the most important dimensions of their own identity. Stereotypes are examined as participants share stories about when they were proud to be part of a particular group and when it was especially hurtful to be associated with a particular group.

Preparation: Circles of My Multicultural Self

This activity highlights the multiple dimensions of our identities. It addresses the importance of individuals self-defining their identities and challenging stereotypes.

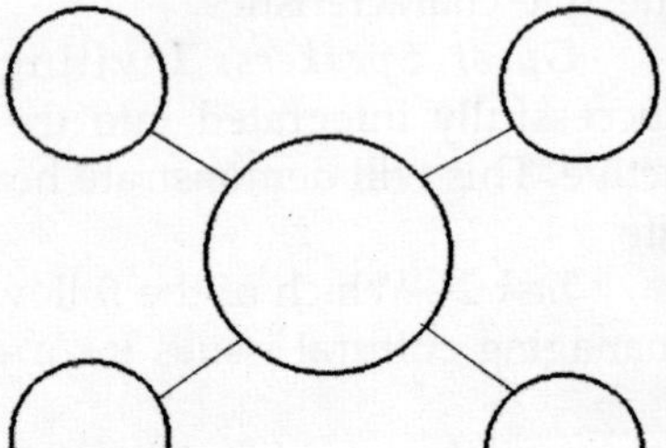

Place your name in the center circle of the structure below. Write an important aspect of your identity in each of the satellite circles—an identifier or descriptor that you feel is important in defining you. This can include anything: Asian American, female, mother, athlete, educator, Taoist, scientist, or any descriptor with which you identify.

1. Share a story about a time you were especially proud to identify yourself with one of the descriptors you used above.
2. Share a story about a time it was especially painful to be identified with one of your identifiers or descriptors.
3. Name a stereotype associated with one of the groups with which you identify that is not consistent with who you are. Fill in the following sentence:

I am (a/an) ________________________ but I am NOT (a/an)______________________.

(So if one of my identifiers was "Christian", and I thought a stereotype was that all Christians are radical right Republicans, my sentence would be:

I am a Christian, but I am NOT a radical right Republican.

Instructions

Ask participants to pair up with somebody they do not know very well. Invite them to introduce each other, then follow these steps:

1. Ask participants to write their names in the center circle. They should then fill in each satellite circle with a dimension of their identity they consider to be among the most important in defining themselves. Give them several examples of dimensions that might fit into the satellite circles: female, athlete, Jewish, brother, educator, Asian American, middle class, etc.
2. In their pairs, have participants share two stories with each other. First, they should share stories

about when they felt especially proud to be associated with one of the identifiers they selected. Next, they should share a story about a time it was particularly painful to be associated with one of the identity dimensions they chose.

3. The third step will be for participants to share a stereotype they have heard about one dimension of their identity that fails to describe them accurately. Ask them to complete the sentence at the bottom of the handout by filling in the blanks: "I am (a/an) ___________ but I am NOT (a/an) ___________."

   Provide your own example, such as "I am a Christian, but I am NOT a radical right Republican." Instructions for steps 1, 2, and 3 should be given at once. Allow 8-10 minutes for participants to complete all three steps, but remind them with 2 minutes remaining that they must fill in the stereotype sentence.
4. Probe the group for reactions to each other's stories. Ask whether anyone heard a story she or he would like to share with the group. (Make sure the person who originally told the story has granted permission to share it with the entire group.)
5. Advise participants that the next step will involve individuals standing up and reading their stereotype statement. You can either simply go around the room in some order or have people randomly stand up and read their statements. Make sure that participants are respectful and listening actively for this step, as individuals are making themselves vulnerable by participating. Start by reading your own statement. This part of the activity can be extremely powerful if you introduce it energetically. It may take a few moments to start the flow of sharing; so allow for silent moments.
6. Several questions can be used to process this activity:
   1. How do the dimensions of your identity that you chose as important differ from the

dimensions other people use to make judgments about you?

2. Did anybody hear somebody challenge a stereotype that you once bought into? If so, what?
3. How did it feel to be able to stand up and challenge your stereotype?
4. (There is usually some laughter when somebody shares common stereotype such as "I may be Arab, but I am not a terrorist" or "I may be a teacher, but I do have a social life.") I heard several moments of laughter. What was that about?
5. Where do stereotypes come from?
6. How can we eliminate them?

Facilitator Notes

The key to this activity is the process of examining one's own identity and the stereotypes associated with that identity, then having one's own stereotypes challenged through others' stories and stereotype challenges. Encourage participants to think about the stereotypes they apply to people and to make a conscious effort to think more deeply about them, eventually eliminating them. As with most activities, it can be especially effective if you participate while you facilitate. If you are willing to share your own experiences, participants are more likely to feel open to share their own.

It is crucial, especially for the final part of the activity when participants are sharing their stereotypes, to allow for silences. People will be hesitant to share initially, but once the ball starts rolling, the activity carries a lot of energy. Allow time at the end for participants to talk more about whatever stereotype they shared. After everyone has shared their stereotype challenge, announce that anyone who would like to share another one can do so. Model by sharing another one about yourself.

Do Some Research

Some of the greatest lessons to be learned in the TESL/TEFL classroom will be learned by the teacher and will be about cultural awareness. You will make mistakes but it is best to apologies and explain that you did not realize it was a cultural misunderstanding. Remember that cultures are different from each other but that there is no correct or right culture. For success it is in your favour as an instructor to conduct some research and enhance the overall level of understanding.

Teaching with Modern Teaching Tools

TECHNOLOGICAL UNDERSTANDING

Technological revolution is changing the face of education worldwide; computers have played a major role in connecting the world. Role of technology in the classroom learning environment has brought drastic changes in the curriculum development and teaching methodologies. As a system computing and tools for learning, teaching and classroom management are gaining more authority and user-friendliness in the teaching fraternity but still disliked by those who don't want to change.

Use of technology in classrooms is a topic, which has given birth to different schools of thoughts: As human beings we don't like change, every teacher is familiar with the use of computers in the classroom, and those who have basic or no formal training in computers, they prefer to keep these exceptionally useful machines out of their classes. Some instructors are taking up technology unequivocally, whereas others feel perplexed, it is imperative for the prospective instructors to be aware of the benefits of the technology. Every instructor must have some basic awareness about the issues, which help in understanding the use of technology.

Keeping in mind the technological revolution instructors should encourage students in learning the basic use of different technological equipments and computers in general. With the changes in the education policy around the world, it is assumed that learners will be gaining knowledge at the same time as they'll be learning about technology. Technology involves using all the language modes as well as viewing and producing to communicate and learn.

By working in pairs and small groups, students can work as a group with other learners to practise important aspects of language vocabulary, which is significant for learning technology. We all know that it is time and again a good idea to mix different level of students, instructors should monitor how relationships are working in the group and they should provide guidance to all learners on group dynamics and how to work cooperatively.

Learners from few cultures especially from Asian and Middle Eastern countries are often not aware and comfortable with group working. Looking at the situation and comfort level of the learner it is the responsibility of the instructor to find out what is helpful for these learners and what kind of assistance should be provided to them. At times, grouping Asian learners with a shared first language and can be a good strategy, this method allows the learners to use the first language to clarify new concepts and develops a level of confidence.

Instructors need to take decisions for the benefit of individual learners and the demands of tasks when putting adult learners into groups. Placing learners in miniature groups and cautiously outlining tasks can help adult learners gain important knowledge and practice from activities while altering key terms and the technology involved. It is a well-known fact that a picture is worth thousand words and this concept works very well in favour of the learners.

Technological Knowhow

Technological knowhow tends to be content specific, reasonably priced and somewhat formal. It uses a large number of technical terms and expressions not used in on a daily basis situations. Learners need to learn most of these terms while developing the language skills—oral and written—to categorize, evaluate, recapitulate, compare, describe, infer, hypothesise, describe and elucidate.

In view of the concerns raised by instructors it is better for us to explore the issues of prime importance that have a direct and indirect impact on the teaching and learning experience of both the instructor and the learners. The essential questions related to the integration of technology and languages are as follows:

- How will technology enhance teaching and learning?
- What should be considered when teaching with technology?
- What are the effects of technology on teaching?

For better understanding of this issue we have to explore the above-mentioned questions in detail and we have to make it clear to all of the present English language instructors and the prospective instructors that technology has to be integrated with language learning and without the use of technology effective language learning is not possible these days.

CAN TECHNOLOGY ENHANCE TEACHING AND LEARNING?

Different schools of thoughts have provided different philosophies both in favour and against using technology. We have to accept the basic reality that technology can make increased learning efficiency doable if it is combined with changes in pedagogy and implementation of different skills. Technology, especially learner-centered technology, can activate principles of learning theory on both the cognitive and the metacognitive levels (Bonk & Cummingham, 1998).

Teaching with technology is dependent upon the familiarity of the instructor with the use of technology and awareness of the instructor with regards to language acquisition and language teaching. When an instructor develops a technology-centered learning atmosphere that places tools in the hands of learners to build, browse, link, juxtapose, represent, and summarize information, the learners are engaged in an intentional process of constructing meaning from information and experience.

Technology enhanced learning environments can also have a positive influence on learner motivation, through factors such as novelty, curiosity, control, personal choice, and effort. These technologies can allow instructors to branch out course content so that learners are exposed to materials from cultures and perspectives different from their own.

Wager and McCombs (1995) summarize the potential benefits of technology-enhanced instructional environments. Such environments can provide greater opportunities for understanding learning activities that are internally driven and constructed, goal-oriented and reflective, personally meaningful and adaptive to individual needs and cultural backgrounds.

When taking into account technology in their teaching, many instructors begin with questions about a variety of technology tools: should I use PowerPoint? Do I need to create a course web page? Would it be easy for learners to log onto the blackboard? What programs are best for getting started? What speed should I take and should I expect wonders in the early stage of the course? Sometimes it is difficult for the instructor to decide which way he or she wants the course to go, while introducing parts of technology into it. Large number of instructors are concerned with the use and importance being given to technology these days, they have talked about it and even now various groups want to keep technology out of the language classes, which doesn't seem that easy now.

From a systems approach, teaching with technology involves four major components: the learners, the instructor, course content, and technology tools. An examination of each component raises a set of issues that we need to think in order to make technology integration as triumphant as possible. When considering any technology tools for instruction, you need to examine your instructional goals: What do you expect learners to learn from the class? What skills and knowledge do you want them to acquire by the end of the term? What teaching strategies will best help students achieve these goals?

Once you have answers to these questions, you can choose the appropriate technologies to prop up your goals and create apposite learning activities to incorporate those technologies into your course. When learning objectives are at the knowledge level (Bloom, 1956), you may use technology tools that support information delivery that reinforce and help apply the knowledge that learners have learned. On the other hand, when the instructional goals are at the analysis/evaluation levels (Bloom, 1956), it is appropriate to provide learners with a complex technology-enhanced learning environment, in which they can apply, integrate, and make sense of what they have learned. Before moving into details related to teaching with technology you must try to think about the following questions about your participants and must spend some time on thinking about the commonly heard assumptions about teaching and learning.

HYPOTHESIS ABOUT TEACHING AND LEARNING

Learners learn best when they use knowledge as a medium for studying content, not when knowledge coaching is presented without a meaningful context.

- Inspiration is the single most significant element for victorious learning for all learners.
- Learners each have exceptional acquaintance and skills, which can be shared to the benefit of both groups.

It is important for instructor to inform the learners about the various ways in which they can use a computer. As an instructor you must tell your learners that if they want to be successful then it is better for them to learn the basic computer skills. First of the instructors have to tell themselves the following:

- Nobody is born knowing everything.
- You have forgotten what it is like to be beginner.
- Knowledge of the learners about the computers is grounded in what they can do and see. Learners need

to develop a deeper understanding of the important and useful computing concepts. Awareness and comprehension takes time, as it is a slow process. Learners will learn by practically doing rather than by the reading different theories.

- As an instructor you must remember that by the time the learners ask you for help, they might have probably tried several different things.
- Teamwork is the best way to learn computer and other technology related skills. Try to use apprenticeship as it one of best way of doing some real task together with someone who has skills that you don't have.
- As an instructor keep in mind that you are a facilitator and your goal is not to solve your learner's problem. Your goal is to help them become independent and more capable of solving their problem on their own.
- Learning a language and then learning a computer might not be easy for each and every learner. Instructor must realise that knowledge lives in communities, not in individuals. A learner who is not part of community of computer users is going to have a harder time of it than one who is.
- Instructor shouldn't take the keyboard in hand and must allow the learners to type, no matter how slow they type, and it is your responsibility as an instructor to encourage them.

The position of technology as a resource for tutoring of second language learners is escalating, as educators know its ability to craft both self-regulating and mutual learning environments in which learners can attain and practice a new language.

With the revolution and increasing use of technology information is available to the learner on a click away. Through the use of the Internet, word processors, multimedia, and practice programs, learners can connect in individualized tutoring designed to meet their explicit needs and contribute in supportive projects that encourage communication with peers in their classrooms and throughout the worldwide community.

Research in second language acquisition (Krashen, 1989) has clearly suggested the need of lucid input in order for second language education to take place. Perhaps the single most significant role of the second language instructor is to act as a facilitator in providing this exhaustive contribution. Conventionally, instructors have relied profoundly on the use of pictures, realia, and gestures to put across meaning to beginning learners.

The computer with its Internet capabilities is a powerful addition to the second language instructor's resources. Computers utilize a multi-sensory collection of text, sound, pictures, and video to provide meaningful contexts to facilitate understanding. Technology is uniformly significant in the sheltered, academic-area classrooms where its capability to provide understandable input serves as a gibbet to support learners as they study rationally challenging subject matter.

While anxiety and lack of inspiration can hinder language learning by acting as filters blocking understanding (Krashen, 1989), technology can help instructors in creating a compassionate affective atmosphere in the classroom. The indefatigable, non-judgmental nature of the computer makes it an ideal instrument to help second language learners feel adequately protected to make and correct their own errors without humiliation.

Technology can provide learners with language experiences as they move through the various stages of language acquisition. Opening with the use of multimedia to provide understandable input in the pre-production or silent period, learner's progress to software's that require limited responses, and in the more advanced stages use their second language as they manoeuvre technology to solve a crisis.

Journalism writing classes have utilized technology to maintain the writing process approach. Computer-generated prompts, outlines, and other graphic organizers can be used for brainstorming. On-line databases offer learners access to information on unrestrained topics. Writing pen pals via electronic mail or chatting on the World Wide Web provides learners with dependable audiences that serve as enthusiasm for revising and editing their writing.

Desktop publishing has provided learners an opportunity to show a sense of pride of possession and build self-esteem as learners publish striking papers and reports. Reliable evaluation is doable through a compilation of learner work in electronic portfolios. Although most drill and practice programs have the weakness of focusing on form over task, such software can be precious in strengthening class instruction and providing focused practice of specific skills. Articulation programs allow second language learners to visually contrast the voice patterns of their speech with that of a native speaker. It is noted and often seen that drill and practice software can be programmed to acclimatize to the language expertise level of each learner, supplying curative guidance and self-paced rehearsal in grammar and vocabulary enlargement.

The technology-enhanced syllabus employs numerous modalities to meet the needs of learners with dissimilar learning styles and strategies. The auditory, ocular, perceptible and kinaesthetic learners have access to a multiplicity of computer-based activities that are well appropriate to their chosen learning styles. As learners perform diverse tasks with the computer, they thicken their catalogue of metacognitive, cognitive, and emotional learning strategies.

The benefits of computer-based technology for second language teaching comprise a convincing squabble for inclusive teacher training in the classroom use of technology. Research, however, suggests that colleges and universities continue to produce teachers who do not have adequate skills in utilizing computers for instructional purposes (Dell and Disdier, 1994; Woodrow, 1993). Moreover, there is growing evidence that second language learners have less access to technology-enriched instruction than native English speakers (Hunt and Pritchard, 1993, Skeele, 1993).

Just say the word technology and you will incite a wide range of responses from that of a super keen computer fan to that of an anxious computer cynic The topic of technology, which has almost become identical with that of computers, is so hot right now it is almost in danger of becoming overdone. While some educators have embraced it and others remain cautious and weary. The second language classroom is not exempted from involvement in this hi-tech wave but questions are still being asked as to the exact role of the computer in this meticulous learning atmosphere.

Why use computers? Though in the nineties this question may appear unenlightened or uninformed, many second language instructors are still moderately debating the justification for their usage. One of the most often mentioned reasons for their introduction to the second language classroom is motivation (Flewelling, 1994). Shrum and Glisan (1994) echo this rationale by saying that children generally have positive attitudes toward technology. So, children like computers. Is that motive sufficient to use them for teaching languages? Perhaps not but it does make the point that learners need to consider interests of their learners as well as existing trends in culture when planning second language curriculum.

Educators, who study and who have studied this scrupulous area of second language learning, agree that the computer is a means to assist and develop the second language learning process and not a new approach to second language teaching in itself. Shrum and Glisan (1994) bear this attitude saying, "CALL (Computer Assisted Language Learning) serves as a supplement or enrichment rather than a substitute for regular classroom learning." It seems that the key to combining this kind of expertise in the second language classroom is to cautiously opt computer-related actions that support the forthcoming methodologies used by most second language teachers. On this point Tracey Forrest states that technology "will only serve teaching goals to the extent that teachers continue to be responsible for their thoughtful and meaningful implementation." (1993, p. 318).

Technology though comprehensive of computers is not totally related to this particular "machine". The use of television, radio, overhead and slide projectors have already gained their fair place in the language classroom as valuable and essential tools. Some instructors feel rather under equipped to execute it in an effectual, meaningful way and to stay on top of this continuously embryonic technology. In 1988, Leblanc & Guberman emphasized a requirement for instructor training in this area and this need remains unfulfilled till this date. Technology is in a steady state of development; it is sometimes difficult to keep in progress. Despite these hurdles, instructors are finding opportunities to determine the potential strength and usefulness of the computer, as it is now a permanent fixture in our world.

THE INSTRUCTOR

Instructor has a great responsibility on his or her shoulders; it is the personality and skills of the instructor, which motivate learners in gaining new skills. As an instructor once you have an apparent observation of the course content and how technology can hold your instructional goals, you will need to ask some questions about your own skills and attitudes:

- How skilled and experienced are you in using technology?
- How do you think of your role as an instructor?
- How much time do you have for course planning and preparation?

Instructors who are efficient in use of technology and who have good experience in using technology, they might not have any difficulty in working in a technology—rich environment even if the course goal doesn't support such a technology-oriented shift. If you have moderately less experience using technology, it might not make sense to move to technology-rich atmosphere even if your course goals would support a shift.

As an instructor if you are not comfortable with the technology then you should seek out support from colleagues in your department, as well as from instructional technology support offices on your campus. You might find out what tools your colleagues are using in their course, what skills you will need to develop in order to be comfortable teaching with this technology, and what workshops are available to support your efforts.

IMPLEMENTING THE SEVEN PRINCIPLES: TECHNOLOGY AS LEVER

by Arthur W. Chickering and Stephen C. Ehrmann

This article originally appeared in print as: Chickering, Arthur and Stephen C. Ehrmann (1996), "Implementing the Seven Principles: Technology as Lever," *AAHE Bulletin*, October, pp. 3-6.

See the bottom of this Web page for updates, a link to a huge collection of ideas for using technology to implement the seven principles, a recorded interview with Chickering and Ehrmann about this history of the seven principles and their relevance to technology use, and our request that you share more such examples of technology use.

In March 1987, the *AAHE Bulletin* first published "Seven Principles for Good Practice in Undergraduate Education." With support from Lilly Endowment, that document was followed by a Seven Principles Faculty Inventory and an Institutional Inventory (Johnson Foundation, 1989) and by a Student Inventory (1990). The Principles, created by Art Chickering and Zelda Gamson with help from higher education colleagues, AAHE, and the Education Commission of the States, with support from the Johnson Foundation, distilled findings from decades of research on the undergraduate experience.

Several hundred thousand copies of the Principles and Inventories have been distributed on two- and four-year campuses in the United States and Canada. (Copies are available at cost from the Seven Principles Resource Center, Winona State University, PO Box 5838, Winona, MN 55987-5838; Ph. 507/457-5020.) — Eds.

Since the Seven Principles of Good Practice were created in 1987, new communication and information technologies have become major resources for teaching and learning in higher education. If the power of the new technologies is to be fully realized, they should be employed in ways consistent with the Seven Principles. Such technologies are tools with multiple capabilities; it is misleading to make assertions like "Microcomputers will empower students" because that is only one way in which computers might be used.

Any given instructional strategy can be supported by a number of contrasting technologies (old and new), just as any given technology might support different instructional strategies. But for any given instructional strategy, some technologies are better than others: Better to turn a screw with a screwdriver than a hammer — a dime may also do the trick, but a screwdriver is usually better.

This essay, then, describes some of the most cost-effective and appropriate ways to use computers, video, and telecommunications technologies to advance the Seven Principles.

1. Good Practice Encourages Contacts Between Students and Faculty

Frequent student-faculty contact in and out of class is a most important factor in student motivation and involvement. Faculty concern helps students get through rough times and keep on working. Knowing a few faculty members well enhances students' intellectual commitment and encourages them to think about their own values and plans.

Communication technologies that increase access to faculty members, help them share useful resources, and provide for joint problem-solving and shared-learning can usefully augment face-to-face contact in and outside of class meetings. By putting in place a more "distant" source of information and guidance for students, such technologies can strengthen faculty interactions with all students, but especially with shy students who are reluctant to ask questions or challenge the teacher directly. It is often easier to discuss values and personal concerns in writing than orally, since inadvertent or ambiguous non-verbal signals are not so dominant. As the number of commuting part-time students and adult learners increases, technologies provide opportunities for interaction not possible when students come to class and leave soon afterward to meet work or family responsibilities.

The biggest success story in this realm has been that of time-delayed (asynchronous) communication. Traditionally, time-delayed communication took place in education through the exchange of homework, either in class or by mail (for more distant learners). Such time-delayed exchange was often a rather impoverished form of conversation, typically limited to three conversational turns:

1. The instructor poses a question (a task).
2. The student responds (with homework).
3. The instructor responds some time later with comments and a grade.

The conversation often ends there; by the time the grade or comment is received, the course and student are off on new topics.

Now, however, electronic mail, computer conferencing, and the World Wide Web increase opportunities for students and faculty to converse and exchange work much more speedily than before, and more thoughtfully and "safely" than when confronting each other in a classroom or faculty office. Total communication increases and, for many students, the result seems more intimate, protected, and convenient than the more intimidating demands of face-to-face communication with faculty.

Professor Norman Coombs reports that, after twelve years of teaching black history at the Rochester Institute of Technology, the first time he used email was the first time a student asked what he, a white man, was doing teaching black history. The literature is full of stories of students from different cultures opening up in and out of class when email became available. Communication also is eased when student or instructor (or both) is not a native speaker of English; each party can take a bit more time to interpret what has been said and compose a response. With the new media, participation and contribution from diverse students become more equitable and widespread.

2. Good Practice Develops Reciprocity and Cooperation Among Students

Learning is enhanced when it is more like a team effort than a solo race. Good learning, like good work, is collaborative and social, not competitive and isolated. Working with others often increases involvement in learning. Sharing one's ideas and responding to others' improves thinking and deepens understanding.

The increased opportunities for interaction with faculty noted above apply equally to communication with fellow students. Study groups, collaborative learning, group problem-solving, and discussion of assignments can all be dramatically strengthened through communication tools that facilitate such activity.

The extent to which computer-based tools encourage spontaneous student collaboration was one of the earliest surprises about computers. A clear advantage of email for today's busy commuting students is that it opens up communication among classmates even when they are not physically together.

For example: One of us, attempting to learn to navigate the Web, took a course taught entirely by a combination of televised class sessions (seen live or taped) and by work on a course Web page. The hundred students in the course included persons in Germany and the Washington, DC area.

Learning teams helped themselves "learn the plumbing" and solve problems. These team members never met face-to-face. But they completed and exchanged Myers-Briggs Type Inventories, surveys of their prior experience and level of computer expertise, and brief personal introductions. This material helped teammates size one another up initially; team interactions then built working relationships and encouraged acquaintanceship. This kind of "collaborative learning" would be all but impossible without the presence of the media we were learning about and with.

3. Good Practice Uses Active Learning Techniques

Learning is not a spectator sport. Students do not learn much just sitting in classes listening to teachers, memorizing prepackaged assignments, and spitting out answers. They must talk about what they are learning, write reflectively about it, relate it to past experiences, and apply it to their daily lives. They must make what they learn part of themselves.

The range of technologies that encourage active learning is staggering. Many fall into one of three categories: tools and resources for learning by doing, time-delayed exchange, and real-time conversation. Today, all three usually can be supported with "worldware," i.e., software (such as word processors) originally developed for other purposes but now used for instruction, too.

We've already discussed communication tools, so here we will focus on learning by doing. Apprentice-like learning has been supported by many traditional technologies: research libraries, laboratories, art and architectural studios, athletic fields. Newer technologies now can enrich and expand these opportunities. For example:

- Supporting apprentice-like activities in fields that themselves require the use of technology as a tool, such as statistical research and computer-based music, or use of the Internet to gather information not available in the local library.
- Simulating techniques that do not themselves require computers, such as helping chemistry students develop and practice research skills in "dry" simulated laboratories before they use the riskier, more expensive real equipment.
- Helping students develop insight. For example, students can be asked to design a radio antenna. Simulation software displays not only their design but the ordinarily invisible electromagnetic waves the antenna would emit. Students change their designs and instantly see resulting changes in the waves. The aim of this exercise is not to design antennae but to build deeper understanding of electromagnetism.

4. Good Practice Gives Prompt Feedback

Knowing what you know and don't know focuses your learning. In getting started, students need help in assessing their existing knowledge and competence. Then, in classes, students need frequent opportunities to perform and receive feedback on their performance. At various points during college, and at its end, students need chances to reflect on what they have learned, what they still need to know, and how they might assess themselves.

The ways in which new technologies can provide feedback are many—sometimes obvious, sometimes more subtle. We already have talked about the use of email for supporting person-to-person feedback, for example, and the feedback inherent in simulations. Computers also have a growing role in recording and analyzing personal and professional performances. Teachers can use technology to provide critical observations for an apprentice; for example, video to help a novice teacher, actor, or athlete critique his or her own performance. Faculty (or other students) can react to a writer's draft using the "hidden text" option available in word processors. Turned on, the "hidden" comments spring up; turned off, the comments recede and the writer's prized work is again free of "red ink."

As we move toward portfolio evaluation strategies, computers can provide rich storage and easy access to student products and performances. Computers can keep track of early efforts, so instructors and students can see the extent to which later efforts demonstrate gains in knowledge, competence, or other valued outcomes. Performances that are time-consuming and expensive to record and evaluate—such as leadership skills, group process management, or multicultural interactions—can be elicited and stored, not only for ongoing critique but also as a record of growing capacity.

5. Good Practice Emphasizes Time on Task

Time plus energy equals learning. Learning to use one's time well is critical for students and professionals alike.

Allocating realistic amounts of time means effective learning for students and effective teaching for faculty.

New technologies can dramatically improve time on task for students and faculty members. Some years ago a faculty member told one of us that he used technology to "steal students' beer time," attracting them to work on course projects instead of goofing off. Technology also can increase time on task by making studying more efficient. Teaching strategies that help students learn at home or work can save hours otherwise spent commuting to and from campus, finding parking places, and so on. Time efficiency also increases when interactions between teacher and students, and among students, fit busy work and home schedules. And students and faculty alike make better use of time when they can get access to important resources for learning without trudging to the library, flipping through card files, scanning microfilm and microfiche, and scrounging the reference room.

For faculty members interested in classroom research, computers can record student participation and interaction and help document student time on task, especially as related to student performance.

6. Good Practice Communicates High Expectations

Expect more and you will get it. High expectations are important for everyone—for the poorly prepared, for those unwilling to exert themselves, and for the bright and well motivated. Expecting students to perform well becomes a self-fulfilling prophecy.

New technologies can communicate high expectations explicitly and efficiently. Significant real-life problems, conflicting perspectives, or paradoxical data sets can set powerful learning challenges that drive students to not only acquire information but sharpen their cognitive skills of analysis, synthesis, application, and evaluation.

Many faculty report that students feel stimulated by knowing their finished work will be "published" on the World Wide Web. With technology, criteria for evaluating products and performances can be more clearly articulated by the teacher, or generated collaboratively with students. General criteria can be illustrated with samples of excellent, average, mediocre, and faulty performance. These samples can be shared and modified easily. They provide a basis for peer evaluation, so learning teams can help everyone succeed.

7. Good Practice Respects Diverse Talents and Ways of Learning

Many roads lead to learning. Different students bring different talents and styles to college. Brilliant students in a seminar might be all thumbs in a lab or studio; students rich in hands-on experience may not do so well with theory. Students need opportunities to show their talents and learn in ways that work for them. Then they can be pushed to learn in new ways that do not come so easily.

Technological resources can ask for different methods of learning through powerful visuals and well-organized print; through direct, vicarious, and virtual experiences; and through tasks requiring analysis, synthesis, and evaluation, with applications to real-life situations. They can encourage self-reflection and self-evaluation. They can drive collaboration and group problem-solving. Technologies can help students learn in ways they find most effective and broaden their repertoires for learning. They can supply structure for students who need it and leave assignments more open-ended for students who don't. Fast, bright students can move quickly through materials they master easily and go on to more difficult tasks; slower students can take more time and get more feedback and direct help from teachers and fellow students. Aided by technologies, students with similar motives and talents can work in cohort study groups without constraints of time and place.

Evaluation and the Seven Principles

How are we to know whether given technologies are as useful in promoting the Seven Principles and learning as this article claims? One approach is to look and see, which is the aim of the "Flashlight Project," a three-year effort begun by the Annenberg/CPB Project to develop and share evaluation procedures. The Flashlight Project is developing a suite of evaluation tools that any campus can use to monitor the usefulness of technology in implementing the Seven Principles and the impacts of such changes on learning outcomes (e.g., the student's ability to apply what was learned in the academic program) and on access (e.g., whether hoped for gains in time on task and retention are saving money for the institution and its funders).

[For more about the Flashlight Program, see Stephen Ehrmann's "Asking the Right Questions: What Does Research Tell Us About Technology and Higher Learning?" in the March/April 1995 Change.]

Technology Is Not Enough

The Seven Principles cannot be implemented by technophiles alone, or even by faculty alone. Students need to become familiar with the Principles and be more assertive with respect to their own learning. When confronted with teaching strategies and course requirements that use technologies in ways contrary to the Principles, students should, if possible, move to alternatives that serve them better. If teaching focuses simply on memorizing and regurgitating prepackaged information, whether delivered by a faculty lecture or computer, students should reach for a different course, search out additional resources or complementary experiences, establish their own study groups, or go to the professor for more substantial activities and feedback.

Faculty members who already work with students in ways consistent with the Principles need to be tough-minded about the software—and technology—assisted interactions they create and buy into. They need to eschew materials that are simply didactic, and search instead for those that are interactive, problem-oriented, relevant to real—world issues, and that evoke student motivation.

Institutional policies concerning learning resources and technology support need to give high priority to user-friendly hardware, software, and communication vehicles that help faculty and students use technologies efficiently and effectively. Investments in professional development for faculty members, plus training and computer lab assistance for students, will be necessary if learning potentials are to be realized.

Finally, it is appropriate for legislators and other benefactors to ask whether institutions are striving to improve educational practice consistent with the Seven Principles. Much depends on the answer.

Note: This article draws on Arthur Chickering's participation in "The Future of Face-to-Face and Distance Learning in Post-Secondary Education", a workgroup chaired by W.L. Renwick as part of a larger effort examining The Future of Post-Secondary Education and the Role of Information and Communication Technology: A Clarifying Report, carried out by the Center for Educational Research and Innovation, Organization for Economic Cooperation and Development, Paris: 1993, 1994.

The Flashlight Program is now a part of the non-profit Teaching, Learning, and Technology Group. The TLT Group provides a range of services to help faculty, their institutions, and their programs make more sensible use of technology. About 250 colleges, universities, state boards, and multi-institution projects now subscribe to TLT Group tools or services.

NEW IDEAS, AND ADDITIONAL READING

Stephen C. Ehrmann
Updated January, 2008

The TLT Group has created a large library of teaching ideas, sorted by the seven principles. It's a successor to, and complement to, the article you've just read. There's a smaller, public version of this article and a larger version plus other resources that's available only to the 300+ institutions that subscribe to the TLT/Flashlight Program. To see this TLT/ Seven Principles library of teaching ideas, click here.

My colleague Steve Gilbert has pointed out another way to array these practices for advancing the seven principles: by how hard or easy they are for faculty to learn quickly and for the institution to support.

Steve has spotlighted *low threshold activities*: uses of technology that are (for that faculty member in that institution at that time) quite easy to learn (in seconds or minutes) and easy for the institution to support (even if all faculty want to use technology in that way.) This Web page contains a growing list of references and materials about such activities. We may soon begin development of a library of low threshold activities for each of the seven principles and, if so, we'll need your help, so watch this space!

Other strategies for implementing the seven principles are 'high threshold': they require substantial reorganization and rethinking of faculty roles. Some of these ideas involve course redesign (e.g., the BioCalc course for teaching calculus to biology students at the University of Illinois, Urbana Champaign). Others, even more ambitious, are conscious efforts to change a major (e.g., by institutionalizing problem-based learning) or a whole institution (e.g., Alverno College). Although some of these ideas have succeeded and have made permanent, national changes in higher learning, too many others have flowered briefly and withered, or never flowered at all. Often the very technology that helped spark interest in these ideas was blamed some years later as inadequate, and the reason the innovation had failed. In "Using Technology to Make Large-Scale Improvements in The Outcomes of Higher Education: Learning From Past Mistakes," I suggested that we've failed repeatedly because we've made the same mistakes repeatedly, in the 1970s, 1980s, 1990s, and today. It's time to learn from those errors. This article draws on past experience to suggest a five part strategy for using technology to make valuable, large scale, lasting improvements in who can learn and what they have learned by the time they complete a program in higher education.

Is it true that research has never proved that technology improves learning? I tried to summarize some of the findings that have had the greatest influence on my own thinking in the 1995 article, "Asking the Right Questions: What Does Research Tell Us About Technology and Higher Learning?" in *Change*, The Magazine of Higher Learning, XXVII:2 (March/April), pp. 20-27. This essay gives a brief overview of the evaluation literature on teaching, learning, technology and costs.

Are there articles or web sites that have proven valuable to you and your colleagues that should be added to this list of resources? Please e-mail me your suggestions and explain the value of the resource. I'll add the best of them to this article (which is currently drawing about 4500 readers a month).

Quotable Quotes

Live as if you were to die tomorrow. Learn as if you were to live forever.

—Mahatma Gandhi

For learning to take place with any kind of efficiency students must be motivated. To be motivated, they must become interested. And they become interested when they are actively working on projects which they can relate to their values and goals in life.

—Gus Tuberville, President, William Penn College

I never teach my pupils; I only attempt to provide the conditions in which they can learn.

—Albert Einstein

Common-sense is part of the home-made ideology of those who have been deprived of fundamental learning, of those who have been kept ignorant. This ideology is compounded from different sources: items that have survived from religion, items of empirical knowledge, items of protective skepticism, items culled for comfort from the superficial learning that is supplied. But the point is that common-sense can never teach itself, can never advance beyond its own limits, for as soon as the lack of fundamental learning has been made good, all items become questionable and the whole function of common-sense is destroyed. Common-sense can only exist as a category insofar as it can be distinguished from the spirit of enquiry, from philosophy.

—John Berger, British author, Critic

Some are born with knowledge, some derive it from study, and some acquire it only after a painful realization of their ignorance. But the knowledge being possessed, it comes to the same thing. Some study with a natural ease, some from a desire for advantages, and some by strenuous effort. But the achievement being made, it comes to the same thing.

— Kung Fu Tzu (Confucius)

Those who educate children well are more to be honored than parents, for these only gave life, those the art of living well.

—Aristotle

The smarter the journalists are, better-off society is. For to a degree, people read the press to inform themselves—and the better the teacher, the better the student body.

—Warren Buffett

I am indebted to my father for living, but to my teacher for living well.

—Alexander the Great

Experience is the teacher of all things.

—Julius Caesar

You have to grow from the inside out. None can teach you, none can make you spiritual. There is no other teacher but your own soul.

—Swami Vivekananda

I have come to believe that a great teacher is a great artist and that there are as few as there are any other great artists. Teaching might even be the greatest of the arts since the medium is the human mind and spirit.

—John Steinbeck

A self-taught man usually has a poor teacher and a worse student.

—Henny Youngman

What students lack in school is an intellectual relationship or conversation with the teacher.

—William Glasser

Failure should be our teacher, not our undertaker. Failure

is delay, not defeat. It is a temporary detour, not a dead end. Failure is something we can avoid only by saying nothing, doing nothing, and being nothing.

—Denis Waitley

Fear is not a lasting teacher of duty.

—Marcus Tullius Cicero

I never had to learn English, French and German because I was brought up as all three languages. I had a private French teacher before I even went to school. That helped a lot.

—Karl Lagerfeld

Our government is the potent, the omnipresent teacher. For good or ill it teaches the whole people by its example.

—Timothy McVeign

Vadim was both my teacher and my husband. I placed myself entirely in his hands.

—Brigite Bardot

I really enjoyed hanging out with some of the teachers. This one chemistry teacher, she liked hanging out. I liked making explosives. We would stay after school and blow things up.

—Maya Lin

The parents have a right to say that no teacher paid by their money shall rob their children of faith in God and send them back to their homes skeptical, or infidels, or agnostics, or atheists.

—William Jennings Bryan

The true teacher defends his pupils against his own personal influence. He inspires self-distrust. He guides their eyes from himself to the spirit that quickens him. He will have no disciple.

—Amos Bronson Alcott

That is a secondary teacher conception—the writer as an observer.

—Peter Bichsel

A good teacher can inspire hope, ignite the imagination, and instill a love of learning.

—Brad Henry

While teaching, I also worked undercover in the lower courts by saying I was a young law teacher wanting experience in criminal law. The judges were happy to assist me but what I learned was how corrupt the lower courts were. Judges were accepting money right in the courtroom.

—Samuel Dash

Cultural dominance of middle-class norms prevail in middle-class schools with a teacher teaching toward those standards and with students striving to maintain those standards.

—James S. Coleman

Every child should have a caring adult in their lives. And that's not always a biological parent or family member. It may be a friend or neighbor. Often times it is a teacher.

—Joe Manchin

The processes of teaching the child that everything cannot be as he wills it are apt to be painful both to him and to his teacher.

—Anne Sullivan Macy

The Sunday School teacher talked too much in the way our grade school teacher used to when she told us about George Washington. Pleasant, pretty stories, but not true.

—Frances Farmer

Poetry is a special use of language that opens onto the real. The business of the poet is truth telling, which is why in the Celtic tradition no one could be a teacher unless he or she was a poet.

—Huston Smith

I was a writer. I just wasn't a very good one. I was lucky enough to have a playwriting teacher who told me that I'd be a better actor than I would a playwright.

—Live Schreiber

I decided at age 9, but I was reinforced at age 13 when a teacher told me I had talent. I can't say she really motivated me because I already knew. I knew I had talent. I went to the Jewish community theater and got in plays there. Then I went for the movies.

—Richard Dreyfuss

A garden is a grand teacher. It teaches patience and careful watchfulness; it teaches industry and thrift; above all it teaches entire trust.

—Gerttude Jekyll

Charming women can true converts make, We love the precepts for the teacher's sake.

—George Farquhar

The role of the teacher is to create the conditions for invention rather than provide ready-made knowledge.

—Seymour Papert

I'm the son of an everyman. My father is a teacher. He teaches physics at a boys' school in Sydney.

—Alex O'Loughlin

No voice teacher can be all things to all people. You have to gain information from whatever sources you can. You have to listen.

—Renee Fleming

I should prefer to have a politician who regularly went to a massage parlour than one who promised a laptop computer for every teacher.

—A.N. Wilson

Americanism demands loyalty to the teacher and respect for his lesson.

—Bainbridge Colby

Teaching is the only major occupation of man for which we have not yet developed tools that make an average person capable of competence and performance. In teaching we rely on the "naturals," the ones who somehow know how to teach.

—Peter F. Drucker

We now accept the fact that learning is a lifelong process of keeping abreast of change. And the most pressing task is to teach people how to learn.

—Peter F. Drucker

My country is a country of teachers. It is therefore a country of peace. We discuss our successes and failures in complete freedom. Because our country is a country of teachers, we closed the army camps, and our children go about with books under their arms, not with rifles on their shoulders. We believe in dialogue, in agreement, in reaching a consensus.

—Oscar Arias Sanchez

"Although the teachers or the students are not the same, the person in charge of education is being formed or re-formed as he/she teaches, and the person who is being taught forms him/herself in the process. . . . There is, in fact, no teaching without learning."

—Paulo Freire

"... there is no valid teaching from which there does not emerge something learned and through which the learner does not become capable of recreating and remaking what has been taught."

—Paulo Freire

"I write books to change the world. Perhaps I can only change one little piece of that world. But if I can empower teachers and good citizens to give these children, who are the poorest of the poor, the same opportunity we give our own kids, then I'll feel my life has been worth it."

—Jonathan Kozol

"More important than the curriculum is the question of the methods of teaching and the spirit in which the teaching is given".

—Bertrand Russell

"No man can be a good teacher unless he has feelings of warm affection toward his pupils and a genuine desire to impart to them what he believes to be of value."

—Bertrand Russell

Imparting education not only enlightens the receiver, but also broadens the giver—the teachers, the parents, the friends.

—Amartya Sen

The teacher that I was for decades, and that I still am in a certain way, wondered what was meant by the word education. I was truly dumbfounded at the very thought of dealing with such an essential and extensive subject.

—Abdoulaye Wade

APPENDIX I

INTERNATIONAL TECHNICAL ASSISTANCE AND TRAINING—GRIFFITH UNIVERSITY

Griffith University was established in 1971 as the second university in Brisbane and, following amalgamations with several former colleges of advanced education, now has campuses at six locations in Queensland, the main campus being at Nathan in Brisbane. It has an enrolment of 18,000 with nearly 1,400 international students (7.6%). The University comprises the Faculties of Asian and International Studies, Commerce and Administration, Education, Environmental Sciences, Humanities, Law, Science and Technology, Business and Hotel Management, Arts, Engineering and Applied Science and Nursing and Health Sciences. The Graduate School of Management, the Queensland College of Art and the Queensland Conservatorium of Music are also part of the University

The Mission of the University states:

In the pursuit of excellence in teaching, research and community service, Griffith University is committed to:

- innovation;
- bringing disciplines together;
- internationalisation;
- equity and social justice;
- lifelong learning; and
- for the enrichment of Queensland, Australia and the international community.

Griffith University was selected for a case study on

internationalization in technical assistance and training because, from the outset, *internationalization* has been a core focus of the University. It has given special emphasis to a range of international activities, spearheaded by its *Faculty of Asian and International Studies.* One of its strengths in engaging in technical assistance and training projects has been its ability to draw on the inherent advantages described in its Mission Statement, especially its *interdisciplinary structure*, its emphasis on *innovation* and on the *international* dimension. In keeping with this focus the University has, from the time of its establishment, directed attention to *problem solving for the region*. Its activities in technical assistance and training projects are seen by the University as part of a long-term process where the benefits to the region, and to the University, may not be immediately apparent but develop over time. Furthermore, involvement in these projects often stimulates and broadens the interests of academics in international activities generally.

The University has a history of *innovation* and, in seeking and bidding for projects, it looks for niche opportunities, usually relatively small projects ($A1 to $A10 million) with a limited geographical spread, e.g. the South Pacific. Profit-making on projects is of secondary importance, the main emphasis being to perform the task well, providing extra services where appropriate and so encourage 'repeat' business and develop a good reputation and track record. Merit is seen in collaborative arrangements, including links with regional and New Zealand universities.

Strategy

At the organisational level, the University is well served by its Office for Research and International Projects (ORIP) which, without limiting the initiatives of individual Faculties and Schools, can assist in ensuring quick responses to requests and opportunities in organisational matters, in the provision of additional resources and in monitoring quality assurance processes, including meeting ISO standards. Faculties have a positive attitude to ORIP. The University does not have a commercial arm, the development of contracts and agreements being the responsibility of ORIP.

In addition to the *culture* of the University and the specific provisions in its *Mission Statement*, a significant contributor to the level and success of technical assistance and training programs, and to international activities generally, is the recognition of the importance of *networking, partnerships, personal inter-relationships, track record,* and the need for *flexibility and incentives* for staff engaged in and developing international projects. In several instances the reputation won by senior Griffith academics in countries in the Asia Pacific region has created favourable images about the University which in turn enhances opportunities for Griffith's involvement in international projects.

This case study focuses on two leading project examples—*Health Education in China,* and *Teacher Education in the South Pacific.*

Planning and Evaluation—Health Education in China

Good examples of the way the culture of the University and its academic emphasis on *Environmental Sciences* and on *Asian Studies* have facilitated effective and successful technical assistance and training projects can be found in the work of the School of Environmental Sciences, in particular in Training and Development in Reproductive Health, in Workplace Health Promotion and in Public Health Education.

Health Education in China

Training and Development in Reproductive Health Research

This project aimed to develop reproductive health research capabilities in China. Funded by the Ford Foundation, and in partnership with the All-China Women's Federation (ACWF) it provided a special training program at Griffith University for researchers and potential trainers from ACWF. The objectives and activities were:

- to identify research and training needs in reproductive health in China;
- to select and train four researchers from China, enabling them to train others; and

- to produce three sets of teaching manuals in Chinese for future training purposes.

Important contributing factors to the initiation and success of the project were:

- the special interest of Griffith in internationalization and in China;
- the multi-disciplinary academic structure of the University; and
- the reputations of the academic staff of the School of Environmental Sciences.

Workplace Health Promotion Project in Shanghai

The forming of a collaborative partnership between Queensland's Department of Health and Griffith University, on the one hand, and the Shanghai Public Health Bureau, on the other hand, resulted from the recognition by WHO of the training and research activities of Griffith University and Queensland Health in the field of workplace health promotion and their development of a practical training model and materials.

Facilitated by Griffith University, Queensland and Shanghai formed a unique partnership in workplace health.

The collaboration involves exchange of information and resource material, reciprocal study tours, training workshops and an international conference.

Public Health Education

Griffith University has an international reputation for its work in Public Health Education. Projects, both current and proposed, have attracted the interest of funding organizations such as the Ford Foundation, WHO and AusAID.

Much of the success derives from the publication *Ecological and Public Health: From Vision to Practice*, co-edited and contributed to by Dr Cordia Chu and Dr Rod Simpson of the Faculty of Environmental Sciences. The publication describes an ecological public health model which combines health promotion and environmental health in its teaching and research programs.

Formal links are being forged with overseas universities, such as the Beijing Medical University, designed to build research and training capabilities in health promotion, reproductive health and ecological public health in order to address future environmental and public health needs of Chinese communities in particular and the Asia Pacific region in general.

In the case of the *Workplace Health Promotion Project in Shanghai,* it has built on the established reputation in China of the School of Environmental Sciences and it is important internationally because health promotion is one of the WHO Western Pacific Regional Office's work priorities. The worksite is considered one of the most important settings to promote health and well-being of workers. In Shanghai, an industrial city of 13.5 million people, an important way of promoting health and preventing illness is through the worksites. The Griffith University consultant is a central figure in the WHO regional health promotion program and is the author of *Guidelines for the Development of Health-promoting Workplaces.*

Benefits—Health Education in China

Benefits which flow from the University's technical assistance and training strategies in the field of *Health Education in China* include:

- a beneficial impact on the recipient country (China);
- the Queensland and Australian communities through the interaction of the Chinese trainees with counterparts and groups in Australia;
- the Griffith community by interactions with its staff and students;
- the reputation gained through the increasing numbers of international students coming to Griffith University from the Asia Pacific region to study environmental and community health;
- issues of immediate international importance are addressed;
- lasting links between health workers in China and Australia are made;

- mutual educational benefits to the participating Faculties of Griffith University and the counterpart Chinese Universities; and
- researchers and post-graduate students from Griffith University are provided with international field work experience.

Planning and Evaluation—Teacher Education in the South Pacific

Griffith University's work in technical assistance projects directed to teacher education and human resource development in the South Pacific illustrates how the experience and track record of a successful project can lead to further opportunities.

In 1992 AusAID (AIDAB at that time) funded the *Fiji-Australia Teacher Education Project* and engaged Griffith University as Project Manager (contract value $A4.25 million) for a three year project the primary objective of which was to establish the Fiji College of Advanced Education as an institution providing secondary teacher training, a pre-service training program for Junior Secondary Teachers, and to consolidate the in-service programs for Senior Secondary Teachers.

Griffith University was responsible for the management and implementation of the project which included over forty in-Australia training attachments and nine distance education programs.

The success of this project led to the University being awarded *the Basic Education Management and Teacher Upgrading Project* valued at approximately $A6 million to commence in the second half of 1996. The primary objective is, in conjunction with the Fiji Ministry of Education, to enhance teaching and learning in Fiji junior secondary schools through the strengthening of teaching, the pre-service preparation of teachers, and the strengthening of research and curriculum development in primary schools.

The University's experience in the South Pacific also led to its successful bid in 1996 for the $A1.4 million contract for the *Tuvalu Education Support Project* which aims to assist in the reform of the 'Education for Life' program. The objective is to promote general development while conserving the local culture.

Benefits—Teacher Education in the South Pacific

The benefits which flow from the University's technical assistance and training strategies in the field of teacher education in the South Pacific include:

- education systems in the region are strengthened;
- the University's reputation both in Australia and overseas is enhanced;
- the process of internationalization is enhanced through the exchange of staff and trainees;
- local and regional educational partners are specifically involved; and
- lecturing staff are able to impart to Australian students first-hand experiences of a range of regional education systems and institutions.

APPENDIX 2

TEACHER TRAINING : WHAT WORKS AND WHAT DOESN'T

Innovations and Trends in Latin America*

By Juan Carlos Navarro and Aimee Verdisco

Achieving successful teacher training is highly sensitive to individual contexts, making perennial formulas hard to find. However, six trends in innovation in teacher training have been identified as being common denominators and operating principles in eight best practices case studies. Technology can be a valuable resource to improve and strengthen activities related to some of these trends. For example, courses taken through the Internet can allow teachers to continue with their in-service teaching education at their own pace and on their free time. By sending e-mails and participating in chat rooms, teachers belonging to Brazil's Accelerated program and Peru's PLANCAD exchange ideas, discuss common difficulties and solutions, and networks are able to extend across borders. Teachers can also watch best practices and problems through videos, as the CAPACITAR teachers do on a weekly basis during special meetings designed for teacher discussions.

In an effort to capture these innovations, the Education Unit of the Inter-American Development Bank, with the support in some cases of other sponsors, commissioned the following eight case studies:

- Teacher training in the context of the Accelerated Training Program, a privately initiated program applied in the school systems of several Brazilian states and municipalities (Oliveira, 1998).
- The Program for the Continuing Education of Teachers (PFPD), developed and managed by the school system of Bogota, Colombia (Chiappe and Zuluaga, 1998).
- The *microcentros* for teacher training in rural schools in Chile (Williamson, 1998).
- Teacher training in the context of the Educational Technology Program in Costa Rica, a collaborative effort between the Omar Dengo Foundation and the

Ministry of Education (Anfossi and Fonseca, 1999).

- The Regional Center for Higher Education—ESTIPAC, in Jalisco, Mexico (Limón, 1998).
- The Regional Centers for Teachers, post-secondary institutions providing a new, intensive program of teacher training in Uruguay (Castro, 1999).
- Teacher training in *Fe y Alegría,* a private, publicly supported network of Catholic schools for poor children in Venezuela (Pérez Esclarín, 1998).
- The Teacher Training Program (*Programa de Capacitación Docente,* PLANCAD) in Peru, under the responsibility of the Ministry of Education (Instituto Apoyo, 2000).

Based on an examination of these cases and a review of the relevant literature, we synthesize six promising trends in innovation in teacher training. These trends are common denominators and operating principles that have been identified in all or several of the cases and abstracted from their original programmatic context to become an incarnation of best practice. They are intended to provide a preliminary indication of the methods and mechanisms of teacher training that can be adapted to meet the daily challenges of improving learning in the classroom. They also have to be understood as practical responses to widely perceived failures of conventional teacher training programs—both pre-service and in-service—in Latin America; failures that affect every link in the chain of a training program, from severe shortcomings in the methods used to train teachers—most commonly, by using traditional lecturing to transmit constructivist approaches to teaching—to extremely limited impact on practice in the classroom, in spite of the substantial resources committed to the task.

For purposes of presentation, the trends are intentionally organized. They start with the most generally accepted, applicable and incorporated in literally all programs under consideration and continue in order by decreasing degree of generality.

Trend 1 : Classroom-based Training

The literature dating from the last decade indicates that effective in-service programs are those that focus on the practical needs of teachers in classrooms. This is confirmed by our (admittedly limited) review of innovations in the region. The most basic trend shared by the cases surveyed appears to be that effective teacher training, pre-service or in-service, is classroom-based. The correlation is direct: the sooner student teachers come into contact with real-life situations associated with professional practice, and the longer this contact is maintained, the more effective the training.

Emphasis on classroom practice should not be confused with the abandonment—assuming for a moment that it takes place—of good preparation in subject knowledge. As a trend, the emphasis on classroom practice injects a dose of reality into the training process. The trend contrasts not only with teacher training removed from the realities of the classroom but, above all, with the excesses of endless theoretical courses and modules of pedagogy, educational planning or related subjects that regularly consume the lion's share of teachers' time in pre- and in-service programs. The idea is one of value added: value added in terms of how to apply theoretical knowledge to concrete situations and to the students in the classroom. The emphasis on classroom practice thus complements competency in subject knowledge. It is in this respect that the trend appears in each of the innovations examined here.

Trend 2 : Effective Teacher Education as Continuing Education

All the cases examined for the purposes of this paper tend to blur the distinction between pre-service and in-service training. Pre-service, as noted above, increasingly includes early immersion in classroom practice; in-service, for its part, increasingly is connected to academic institutions that reach beyond their walls to develop close relationships with schools. Two practical implications of these trends emerge:

- Pre-service training tends to become shorter in duration. For example, *the Centros Regionales de*
- *Profesores,* CERPs (post-secondary institutions), a pre-service program recently developed in Uruguay, trains middle and high school level teachers in three years; this compares to the four or even five years now common in most countries in the region. Rather than

offering a program of 20 hours per week stretched over many years, as the traditional system does, CERP is a 40 hours per week program.

- In-service training becomes longer. Rather than a single event, training is seen as a continuous process.

Each of the innovations examined in this study shows definite movement in this direction.

Training is conceived and used as a means for developing teachers' capacity for self-reflection and professional decision-making in the classroom. Such skills lay a foundation for effective teaching. They are applicable regardless of curriculum or student population. Once developed, it is precisely these skills that are reinforced by continuous nurturing.

Trend 3: Group Training and Networking

Most of the innovations reviewed here are organized around work groups. By providing "critical friends" to examine and reflect on teaching and opportunities to share experiences associated with efforts to develop new practices or strategies, these groups—structured as teacher-to-teacher networks—become powerful learning tools. Depending on the composition of the group, the training delivered directly responds to the needs of a particular school and its teachers. For example, *Microcentros* in Chile provide rural teachers with an opportunity to exchange experiences, take on joint projects, and otherwise learn from each other. In much the same vein, rather than pulling together teachers from different schools, training provided through the *Fe y Alegría* system engages groups of teachers in the same school.

In the Accelerated Learning (Brazil) and PLANCAD (Peru) programs, teachers participate in a range of networking activities, including follow-up meetings, e-mail or regular mail exchanges (both countries) and peer-directed meetings (Brazil). Moreover, for those who also have access to the CAPACITAR Program, weekly teacher-directed and focused meetings are used to watch and discuss these videos and the good practices they present.

Trend 4: Intensive Use of Pedagogic Support and Supervision

Supervisory mechanisms lie at the heart of program success in many cases. Supervisors play an active role throughout the training exercises, and supervision, in turn, is used to provide encouragement and constructive feedback. In most instances, supervisors are former teachers, a requirement in the Brazilian, Chilean and Venezuelan cases. The benefits of this arrangement are many: teachers-turned-supervisors assume their tasks with first-hand knowledge of the classroom and of the daily challenges that teachers face. To a large extent, they are able to approach their work as peers and tutors, rather than government bureaucrats or other "outsiders" with limited knowledge and experience of the realities of the teaching profession.

These programs are making major contributions toward a radically new definition of supervision that preserves little, if any, of traditional supervisory practices so common and so often meaningless, repressive or even corrupt in most countries across the region. Under this new definition, supervisor-tutors become key sources of on-site pedagogic support for teachers, both within the school and within the community. Frequently, these new networks clash with more traditional networks of supervisors, producing debilitating effects on the effectiveness of training. Teachers participating in PLANCAD, for example, complain that insofar as regional supervisors do not share their training in new pedagogic approaches, advice regarding good practices in the classroom varies, even conflicts. This serves as a reminder of the difficulties involved with trying to move the pieces of the teacher-training machine in unison.

Trend 5: Integration of Training into the Larger Framework of Teacher Career Regulations and Incentives

Several of the innovations reviewed here include activities to restructure the role of incentives in teacher training programs. In some cases (e.g., the PFPD Program in Colombia), teachers are awarded points only after completing a year long training program pre-approved for content and relevancy. The perverse effect of a "point system", by which teachers end up focusing on the accumulation of certificates with little regard for quality or relevance of the training receive, thus is offset by the strict regulation of the quality and content of the training supplied. In other cases (e.g., *Fe y Alegría* and the CERP Program), training activities are developed in a way consistent with the recruitment and selection practices of school networks.

It is worth noting that this trend crosses the line from quite universally accepted practice into the territory of less than universally accepted or adopted approaches. Indeed, in contrast to the Colombia, Venezuelan and Uruguayan programs, the Accelerated Training Program in Brazil characterizes itself as a "surgical intervention." Operating on the "surface", it leaves all rules and regulations governing schools and the teaching profession in place. To its proponents, this stands out as a virtue. The program can be readily applied without the need for more ambitious and politically difficult educational reforms. These findings are consistent with our basic premise: there is no single best way to solve the complex puzzle of teacher training. What works in Catholic schools for poor children in Venezuela or in the public schools of Bogota may be neither appropriate nor relevant for municipal schools in the Northeast of Brazil where they are battling high rates of repetition. Yet, there is a common denominator. This trend points to a new sophistication on the part of policy-makers to consider and apply incentives. It is underpinned and driven by a strong awareness of counter-productive outcomes that have resulted from the incentives built into traditional teacher training arrangements. It is this awareness, not the particular approach or design of incentives, that each of the cases examined here share.

Trend 6: Training as a Response to Social and Educational Priorities at the Local Level

Several of the innovations share the common trait of being linked closely to their social and educational contexts. The *Microcentros* in Chile, for instance, were conceived at a time when urban schools were receiving strong support through channels that were not appropriate for rural schools. The CERP Program, to cite a further example, was created with the explicit objective of training teachers from and in the country's interior (see ANEP, 1999). The Accelerated Learning Program, for its part, was designed within the context of a larger project to tackle high rates of repetition and their direct consequence, the abundance of overage children in the Brazilian schools. The ESTIPAC Program is designed to meet the needs of rural schools and teachers.

Indeed, those involved in running these programs see this closeness as a key to program effectiveness. Training is effective when the challenges faced in a particular time and place are well understood, the teachers, students and schools toward which training is directed are correctly profiled, and the education system is structured in a way that lends reciprocal support (e.g., from the surrounding community) to the training activities provided.

Conclusion

Each of the programs examined here departs from the same point: a general dissatisfaction with dominant practices in teacher training. In responding to this dissatisfaction, each program combines several trends into viable and effective packages. These packages not only encompass good or new ideas in the field, most of which find support in the broader literature, but also emerge as ideas with concrete consequences on program organization, management, pedagogy and impact. It is worth reiterating that not all trends are universally accepted. At a minimum, they serve to emphasize the fact that there are no fast and ready recipes for teacher training. The challenge is one of getting the right ingredients in every recipe. It is hoped that the trends outlined here provide some indication of what those ingredients may be.

APPENDIX 3

TEACHERS USE TECHNOLOGY IN CLASSROOM CONTROL

New Classroom Technology Used in Effective Classroom Management

By **Marcy Paulson**

Jeff Paulson—an elementary teacher, instructional coach, and educational consultant—works with teachers to improve instructional practice. He has also contracted with the U.S. Department of Education to conduct nationwide professional development for teachers. Many of his effective classroom management techniques are based on a simple principle—if students are offered goals for learning that are authentic and relevant, they will work towards those goals and for the most part avoid spending energy in misbehavior. Here, he shares practical ways technology in classrooms can help teachers design lessons with relevant goals for student learning.

New Classroom Technology, an Asset to Classroom Control

On a typical day, some of Paulson's fourth grade students may be updating the class wiki space by researching an aspect of the current Social Studies unit. Other students are recording their personal narratives as podcasts and uploading them to the school website. Others are conferencing with Paulson before posting persuasive arguments as blogs. And another group uses a Flip camera to record a Science experiment to post as a video podcast.

In Paulson's opinion, new classroom technology is a useful tool, but definitely a means rather than an end. "Technology is not the silver bullet to education," he admits. "There's nothing magical about it, and several studies have shown that simply adding technology to the curriculum will not affect test scores in anyway. As the McKinsey report stated in 2007, 'The only way to improve outcomes is to improve instruction'."

Benefits of Classroom Technology Integration to Classroom Control

Technology—in the right instructional hands—gives students a culturally relevant way to publish their own writing, including text, audio, video, and multi-media. "It is differentiated, it is immediate, and it also provides a forum for feedback, by allowing readers to comment", remarks Paulson.

As any teacher knows, writing is much more than simply putting words together and uploading. There are many things to master: grammar, vivid language, content, and presentation. "It's been my experience", Paulson says, "that students are more motivated to excel in these areas when they get to publish in a way that is real to them. Many students don't like to write and avoid it at all costs. These same students go home and create social networking sites, blogs, and videos for You Tube. They collaborate with other online users in a variety of media. Any teacher that doesn't recognize the value of this is missing a huge opportunity".

Classroom Technology Integration into Relevant Learning

A third grader introduced himself to Paulson a few years ago on registration day by writing down the web address of his YouTube video site. Paulson remembers this as one of his first wake-up calls to the relevancy technology can bring to student learning. "Just like adults", Paulson remarks, "children are motivated to write when they know someone else is going to experience it. They have this innate need to create. And who wants to create or write something if it's not going to be published?"

At that time, Paulson wasn't quite as tech savvy as he is now. On a whim, he asked his students to complete a research project using technology to assemble and present the research. Some students chose to create a web site complete with photos, video, links, and text, one created a podcast, and a few used the internet, digital cameras, and color printers to make a display board for an oral presentation.

"I didn't know enough about creating video for the web or about creating a web site", Paulson laughs. "I probably should have learned a little more about it all before jumping in the deep end of the pool. In a lot of ways, the students forged the path, and I have learned what I'll do differently next year. It reminds me of a quote I heard somewhere. I think Alvin Toffler said, 'The illiterate of the 21st century will not be those who cannot read and write, but those who cannot learn, unlearn, and relearn.'"

Teachers Use Technology in Classroom Control: New Classroom Technology Used in Effective Classroom Management http://teachingtechnology.suite101.com/article.cfm/teachers_use_technology_in_classroom_control#ixzz0bfeMQWTk

Bibliography

Bates, A.W. (1974) Success and Failure in Innovation at the Open University, Programmed Learning and Educational Technology, Vol. 11, No. 1, pp. 16-23.

Blaug, M. (1970/72) An Introduction to the Economics of Education, England. Penguin Books Ltd.

Broadsheets about Distance Education. International Extension College, England. Cambridge University Press.

CIEFL (1987) The Supplementary Note to the Priorities and Strategies of CIEFL, (Mimeograph), Hyderabad.

Conference Papers (1982) Twelfth International Council for Distance Education.

Forrester, J. (1974) Demonstration Lessons English Language Teaching. Vol. 29, No. I.

Lee, W.R. (1974) On Getting Down to Grassroots in EFL Instructor Training. English Language Teaching. Vol. 29, No. 1.

Lord Perry, W. (1974) Educational Technology at the Open University : An Approach to the Problem of Quality. *British Journal of Educational Technology*.

O'Hear (1981) Education, Society and Human Nature, London. Routledge and Kegan Paul.

Singh, B. (1982) Correspondence Education in India. Patiala. NCCE Publication.

Williamson, B. (1979) Education, Social Structure and Development. London. MacMillan.

Bendix, E.H. The Data of Semantic Description. In Steinberg and James, in Press.

Bereiter, Carl, and Engelmann, Siegfried, Teaching Disadvantaged Children in the Pre-school. Englewood Cliffs, N.J.: Prentice-Hall, 1966.

Bernstein, Basil. Aspects of language and learning in the genesis of the social process. In Dell Hymes (Ed.), Language in Culture and Society. New York: Harper and Row, 1964, pp. 251-63.

Bolinger, Dwight. The atomization of meaning. Language, 41, 1965, 555-73. (Also reprinted in James and Miron, 1967.)

Bruner, J.S., Goodnow, J.J., and Austin, C.A., A Study of Thinking. New York: John Wiley, 1957. (Second printing.)

Cherry, Colin. On Human Communication. New York: John Wiley, 1957.

Chomsky, N. Language and Mind. New York: Harcourt, Brace & World, 1968.

Chomsky, N. Aspects of the Theory of Syntax. Cambridge, Mass.: The M. I. T. Press, 1965.

Chomsky, N. Verbal behavior (a review). *Language*, 1959, 35, 26-58. (Also reprinted in James and Miron, 1967.)

Chomsky, N. Syntactic Structures. The Hague: Mouton & Co., 1957.

Christensen, F. The problem of defining a mature style. *English Journal*, 1968, 572-79.

Garfinkel, Harold. Studies in Ethnomethodology. Englewood Cliffs, N.J.: Prentice-Hall, 1968.

Coffman, Erving. Interaction Ritual. Garden City, N.Y.: Doubleday (Anchor Books), 1967.

Goffman, E. The Presentation of Self in Everyday Life. New York: Doubleday, 1959.

Grice, Paul. Meaning. *Philosophical Review*, 56, 1957, 377-388.

Harman, Gilbert. Three levels of meaning. *The Journal of Philosophy*, 65, 1968, 590-602. (Also reprinted in Steinberg and James, in Press.).

Heny, F.W. Semantic operations on base structures. Department of Linguistics, Massachusetts Institute of Technology, 1969. (Mimeo.).

Hunt, K.W. Grammatical Structures Written at Three Grade Levels. Champaign, Ill.: National Council of Teachers of

English, 1965. (Research Report No. 3.) Hymes, Dell. Toward ethnographies of communication. In J.J. Gumperz and Dell Hymes (Eds.), The Ethnography of Communication. *American Anthropologist*, 66, 1964, 1-34.

Hymes, Dell. The ethnography of speaking. In T. Gladwin and W.C. Sturtevant (Eds.), Anthropology and Human Behavior. Washington, D.C.: Anthropological Society, Washington, 1962, pp. 13-53.

James, L.A. Rhetoric and stylistics: Some basic issues in the analysis of discourse. English Composition and Communication, in Press.

———, Some potential uses of the Cross-Cultural Atlas of Affective Meanings. Proceedings of the XI Congress of the Inter-American Society of Psychology, February 1969, No. 40, 1-16. (Originally presented in Mexico City, December 1967).

———, The act of composition: Some elements in a performance model of language. Conference on the Composing Process, Colorado Springs, November 1968. (The National Council of Teachers of English, Champaign, Ill.: Proceedings forthcoming.).

———, Mediation theory and the "single-stage" S-R model: Different? *Psychological Review*, 1966, 73, 376-81.

———, and Miron, M. S. (Eds.) Readings In the Psychology of Language. Englewood Cliffs, N.J.: Prentice-Hall, 1967.

Katz, J.J. The Philosophy of Language. New York: Harper and Row, 1966.

———, and Fodor, J.A. The Structure of a Semantic Theory. *Language*, 39, 1963, 17~210. (Also reprinted in James and Miron, 1967).

Kochman, Thomas. Black English in the Classroom. Department of Linguistics, Northeastern Illinois State College, October 1969. (Mimeo.).

Koen, F.M. (with A.L. Becker and R.E. Young). The Psychological Reality of the Paragraph. In E.M. Zale (Ed.), Proceedings of the Conference on Language and Language Behavior. New York: Appleton-Century-Crofts, 1968.

Kuhn, T.S. The Structure of Scientific Revolutions. Chicago: University of Chicago Press, 1962.

Osgood, C.E., James, L.A., May, W.H., and Miron, M.S. The Structure of Affective Meaning: A Multi-cultural Application of Semantic Differential Technique. (University of Illinois Press, forthcoming).

Osgood, G.E. and Sebeok, T.A. (Eds.) Psycholinguistics: A Survey of Theory and Research Problems. *Journal of Abnormal and Social Psychology, Supplement*, 1954. (Reprinted by Indiana University Press, Bloomington, 1965.)

Osgood, C.E., Suci, G., and Tannenbaum, P.H. The Measurement of meaning. Urbana, III: The University of Illinois Press, 1957. Searle, J.R. Speech Acts: An Essay in the Philosophy of Language. Cambridge, England: Cambridge University Press, 1969.

Skinner, B.F. Verbal Behavior. New York: Appleton-Century-Crofts, 1957.

Slobin, D.I. Universals of grammatical development in children. To appear in G. Flores d'Arcais and W. Levelt (Eds.), Proceedings on the Conference of Psycholinguistics (University of Padova, Italy, July 1969).

Smith, Frank and Miller, G. A. (Eds.) The Genesis of Language: A Psycholinguistic Approach. Cambridge, Mass.: The M.1. T. Press, 1966.

Steinberg, D. and James, L.A. (Eds.) Semantics: An Interdisciplinary Reader in Philosophy, Linguistics, and Psychology. Cambridge, England: Cambridge University Press, in Press.

Tyler, S.A. (Ed.) Cognitive Anthropology. New York: Holt, Rinehart and Winston, 1969.

Index